BEFORE
THE BRAND

BEFORE THE BRAND

CREATING THE UNIQUE DNA
OF AN ENDURING BRAND IDENTITY

ALYCIA PERRY

with David Wisnom III

McGraw-Hill

New York   Chicago   San Francisco   Lisbon   London
Madrid   Mexico City   Milan   New Delhi
San Juan   Seoul   Singapore
Sydney   Toronto

The **McGraw·Hill** Companies

1 2 3 4 5 6 7 8 9 0   AGM/AGM   0 9 8 7 6 5 4 3 2

ISBN 0-07-139309-9

McGraw-Hill books are available at special discounts to use as premiums and sales
promotions, or for use in corporate training programs. For more information,
please write to the Director of Special Sales, Professional Publishing, McGraw-Hill,
Two Penn Plaza, New York, NY 10121-2298. Or contact your local bookstore.

 This book is printed on recycled, acid-free paper containing
a minimum of 50% recycled, de-inked paper.

Library of Congress Cataloging-in-Publication Data

Perry, Alycia.
    Before the brand : creating the unique DNA of an enduring brand
identity / by Alycia Perry and David Wisnom III.
        p. cm.
    Includes bibliographical references and index.
        ISBN 0-07-139309-9 (acid-free)
    1. Brand name products.   2. Brand name
    products—Marketing—Management.   3. Trademarks—Design.
    4. Advertising—Brand name products.   I. Wisnom, David. II. Title.
    HD69.B7 P477 2003
    658.8′27—dc21

                                                    2002152803

Dedication

For all the people who create brands
and keep their sense of humor.

Acknowledgments from Alycia

My profound thanks to all the people in my life who enabled this book to be written including my family, friends, and spiritual kins of the 13th Moon Mystery School Kivas. My entrée into product development was thanks to a little company called DFS and particularly Ian Williams. My entrée into brand identity was thanks to Landor and particularly Jean-Marc Bara, Dave Hurlbert, Brett Mangels, Hayes Roth, and Lia Nikopoulou—all of whom I appreciate and admire and thank for believing in me. Love and thanks to my colleagues who let me bend their ears more often than not over the years as both colleagues and friends: Jeff Marcus, Mel Owen, Dean Fernandes, Cynthia Johnston, Tania Leach, Dave, and Lia. And of course special thanks to David Wisnom III for believing in the ability to do it all differently. Thank you, Fire Sparkles The Sky.

CONTENTS

PREFACE

My inspiration to write this book was largely a selfish one. Over the years I was increasingly surprised at how little information about the basics of brand identity is available to the business community. It seemed that because I am both a naming and brand identity consultant, education about the basics was much of my job, which frankly made much of the identity creation process more difficult and time-consuming to complete and implement. The fact that the media and many agencies themselves changed the definition of "branding" to mean advertising, marketing, P.R., and everything else related to brand building made the task all the more challenging. I felt frustration more often than not that no one could say the words *brand* or *branding* and mean the same thing.

Which brings us to the purpose of this book: to identify and clarify the basics of brand identity. *Before the Brand* is written about what comprises a brand identity and provides an overview of how to create an effective and enduring identity before the identity is built via advertising, P.R., marketing, etc. Whether managers and executives take on this task in-house or look to outside consultants to create or redefine an identity, the contents herein provide a primer of brand identity knowledge and process. It's my hope that managers and executives benefit from the knowledge so that stronger and more relevant identities are created and built over time. Therefore, we all win.

Alycia Perry

1

IDENTITY ABCs

Once upon a time, a long, long time ago, artisans marked walls and wares to establish who owned or made something. The walls of the Lascaux caves in southern France contain not only painted bison but also handprints—a form of ownership marking. It's believed that these handprints date to around 15,000 B.C. The ancient Egyptians, Greeks, Romans, and Chinese used seals to mark pottery and other wares to indicate both ownership and quality. If people loved the item, they knew who to praise and buy from in the future. And if there was a problem, they also knew who was responsible. Somewhere along the way, governments decided these markings were a very good thing to have on products—not so much because they were champions of consumer knowledge but because it was much easier to collect taxes when products were marked. In 1266, England passed the Bakers Marking Law, which required stamps or pinpricks on loaves of bread to indicate origin. Spirit makers marked their oak barrels of scotch whiskey with a hot iron symbol to indicate the liquor's origins. Yes, it was nice to know which distillery had produced the whiskey, but in truth customs and excises would have it no other way. These markings are some of the first modern occurrences of the commercial brand.

Fast-forward a few centuries and we find ourselves in an age inundated by brands. No longer is a brand merely a burnt-iron mark of origin or pinpricks on a loaf of bread. It has a name, subnames, color, graphic design, sound, vocabulary, and experience. It has its own identity. No longer is the brand seen only in warehouses or store shelves. It's sent out by satellite, network servers, and printing empires to audiences around the world. The identity acquires an animated life to become a three-dimensional image in the consumer's mind.

What is a brand? A brand is a promise of a relationship and a guarantee of quality. It establishes a relationship between a company and its audiences. A strong brand can and will

- Differentiate
- Create a preference
- Command a premium

A strong brand is the badge, emblem, and global symbol that can bestow credibility and attract instant attention in a new country, category, or industry. It's a powerful way to stand out by being relevant to target audiences and different from the competition. (Please note we stated relevant, then different—and not the other way around.) A brand can be a company, a product, or a service. And since the onset of the high-tech interactive age, it can also be an underlying technology or even a conference.

A brand is all-encompassing. Much like a person, a brand has a fundamental identity, a projected image, perceptions about it held by others, and relationships to parents, siblings, and those we want to get to know and impress.

Identity versus Image

Identity and image—the two go hand in hand, and yet thanks to the late rush at the end of the last century, the two terms are completely misused and misunderstood. Whether it's identity, image, brand, brand building, or another "brand" variation, a new generation of journalists, agencies, and consultants have used these terms to mean just about anything and everything.

Part of the present dilemma is human nature. As consumers, we often think of brands as synonymous with the name of that company. Think of Nike, Apple, or Microsoft. These brands evoke a series of thoughts, images, and perceptions that come through our conscious thoughts as one collective impression. It's often difficult to separate a name from its visual identity or from the experience of that particular brand. Nike becomes synonymous with the Nike "Swoosh" and the company's high-tech retail stores, Apple with its once-bit apple and avant-garde computers.

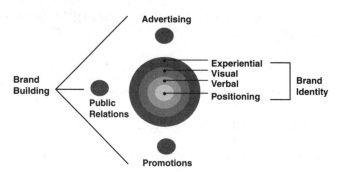

Figure 1–1. The relationship of brand identity and brand building.

For many years, branding simply meant identity. Contrary to what many journalists, agencies, and consultants say, branding does not encompass everything from a name to a banner ad to the kitchen sink. There really and truly is a difference between brand identity and brand building. If you take away one thing from this book, remember this: Without a strong identity, image is nothing. (See Figure 1–1.)

Brand Identity

Think of a brand's identity like that of a person. Initially, a child's identity is made up of a core essence, personality traits, physical traits, a name, and eventually a basic vocabulary. The identity eventually matures with age. Friends and relationships change, interests change slightly or altogether, vocabularies increase, and sometimes even body size and eye and hair color are changed to create a new fundamental look. These changes may range from subtle to radical.

Simply defined, identity is made up of the controllable elements of a company, product, or service brand, such as the core essence, positioning, brand name, tag line, logo, messaging, and experience. These are the fundamental elements that are established to stand the course of years, not just the quarterly ad cycle. We say *controllable elements* because any of these elements can be modified at any given point. A company has greater control over creating and fine-tuning the identity, than over creating or changing an image.

Brand Building

Once the identity is created, the company attempts to build the brand through marketing-related activities, such as advertising, public relations, and promotions, in order to capture the attention of intended audiences. In other words the company begins to establish the brand identity in the minds of consumers before consumers have direct experience with the brand itself.

If an identity is established before the brand is built, the brand-building effectiveness becomes much more targeted and efficient. With an actual identity in place, it is much easier to articulate the right message to intended audiences and allows for a strong, consistent, relevant, and differentiated brand. Why? Because the image, once created, is subject to target audiences' perceptions. And perceptions, as we all know, are highly subjective and erratic. This is the point at which companies lose direct control of their brand—once the brand has entered the intended consumer's experience and mind.

Brand Image

If an identity is the fundamental state of being, then image is the state of perception. The brand image is the collection of largely uncontrollable perceptions of that brand as strengths and weaknesses, positives and negatives. These perceptions are created over time through direct and indirect experiences with the brand. Do you like the name? What do you think of the logo? Has your experience at a store, at a Web site, or with a customer service representative been pleasant and beneficial, your worst nightmare, or somewhere in between? What are your perceptions of the brand based on something you read in the *Wall Street Journal* or *Fast Company,* or even *Consumer Reports*?

Any spin doctor will tell you that an image can be masterfully created and deployed, but it is how the image is received and perceived that ultimately determines its final impact. In other words, the audience's perceptions solidify the brand's image. As perceptions fluctuate and change, so does the image.

An Identity Is More Than a Name and Logo

A company's ability to differentiate its corporate, product, or service brands from the competition and be relevant to its customers is critical to its overall success. The strategy behind its positioning, name, and visual identity is the key ingredient to managing the customer's perception of the brand.

As consultants, we preach the concept of relevance all the time. In the late 1990s, dot-coms went to great lengths to be different. Remember the television spots for Canon-flying gerbils and naked entrepreneurs? Maybe. But do you remember which brand those commercials were trying to build? Most likely not.

What Outpost.com, Beyond.com, and others forgot about was that being different from the competition and using the most outlandish measures to prove it, led to obscurity more often than not. We do believe that different is good. A company certainly does not want to be a carbon copy of the competition (the me-too syndrome). However, the place to start in creating and ultimately building an identity is by being relevant first and foremost.

We can illustrate this concept with simple building blocks. The sum of the blocks is what we call *brand relativity*. (See Figure 1–2.)

Brand relevance is how well the brand speaks to individual audiences. The articulation of a brand to its audience should always be relevant to those audience needs and desires, and as we stated, not merely differentiated. *Brand personification* is the multifaceted personality and character of the brand that helps customers identify with it. A person is not made up of just a few common physical and personality traits, so why should a brand be? *Brand assets* include core strengths and weaknesses, what a brand can promise and, taken a step further, what a brand can guarantee. *Brand differentiation* is what

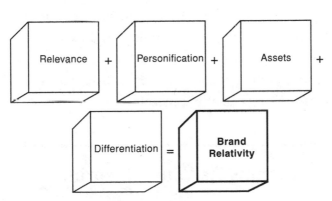

Figure 1–2. The brand relativity equation.

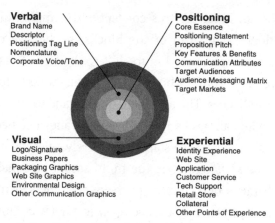

Verbal
Brand Name
Descriptor
Positioning Tag Line
Nomenclature
Corporate Voice/Tone

Positioning
Core Essence
Positioning Statement
Proposition Pitch
Key Features & Benefits
Communication Attributes
Target Audiences
Audience Messaging Matrix
Target Markets

Visual
Logo/Signature
Business Papers
Packaging Graphics
Web Site Graphics
Environmental Design
Other Communication Graphics

Experiential
Identity Experience
Web Site
Application
Customer Service
Tech Support
Retail Store
Collateral
Other Points of Experience

Figure 1–3. Composition of a brand identity.

makes the brand unique, the tangible and intangible traits that set your brand apart. *Brand relativity* as both philosophy and process includes the different components that create the sum of the identity.

A brand identity is broken down into four core areas: positioning, verbal, visual, and experiential. (See Figure 1–3.) Many of these topics are covered in depth in future chapters. Here is a brief overview of these essential identity concepts.

Positioning As Your Blueprint

The term *positioning* is thrown around loosely. What everyone tends to agree on is that a brand must be positioned correctly in the marketplace just to survive. From an identity perspective, positioning is the anchor and sets the tone—be it verbally or visually—for the communication of that company, product, or service. Positioning provides the tactical blueprint that anchors the creative vision to then create an identity. Positioning also clearly communicates to the intended audience what the product, service, or company is about.

While positioning can mean several things to several people, we define it as the sum of distinct components in relationship to the marketplace—meaning direct and indirect competitors. Those components include the proposition pitch, price points, target markets, competitive practices, corporate relationships, target audiences, key features and benefits, audience messaging matrix, communication attributes, core essence, positioning statement, identity objectives, and technical parameters. Depending on the scope and scale of the new identity—a one-product company or a family of products offered by the subsidiary of a parent company—these components may consist of multiple layers and relationships.

As we show in Chapter 2, positioning strategy is not rocket science. Whether you're creating a strategy for a multimillion-dollar global conglomerate or a new product for the parents of toddlers, at the end of the day, what positioning must provide is a unique, ownable (in the sense of being potentially proprietary), and defensible strategy. This is the stage setting for a dynamic, cohesive, and consistent identity.

The Power of the Word

A verbal identity consists of anything that can be spoken or articulated in print. A name, a descriptor, a positioning tag line, and copy points for a brochure or sales sheet are all core components of a verbal identity. The Nike identity is a classic example of a short, evocative name (Nike, the Greek god of victory) and aspirational tag line ("Just Do It"). Together they have extended from product packaging to many types of ads.

The power of words in relation to identities was long ignored by agencies and in-house teams alike. Much of the apathy changed with the dot-com boom. When pioneers such as Yahoo! and Amazon.com hit the scene, a succession of new contenders raced to obtain the hippest, albeit most obscure, names and tag lines. Suddenly words packed a greater, more valuable punch and merited more attention, both financially and creatively.

The importance of words certainly hasn't diminished since the demise of dot-coms. A name and what it immediately communicates is clearly relevant and a top priority. The name is clarified by the generic descriptor, which communicates in everyday language the nature of the product, service, or company—for example, Kleenex *facial tissues*. Positioning tag lines further clarify and reinforce a message, stating who you are, what you do, and why you're unique.

Promotional tag lines do not generally translate to positioning tag lines. Promotional tag lines usually have a short life cycle; they are created with a message intended to promote the company, product, or service descriptively, evocatively, and/or emotionally. Positioning tag lines are created for the long haul. They uniquely position the company, product, or service in one concise statement, communicating to intended audiences what the brand is inherently about.

When Amazon.com was first introduced, the company needed to clarify what it actually did. The word "Amazon" evoked a vast, wild river, not a bookstore. The ".com" portion of the name established its online presence. A portion of Amazon.com's brand success is attributable to the name's exotic imagery along with the key communication point of the biggest river on the planet. To enhance that point, and clearly communicate what the company offered, the company devised the tag "The World's Largest Bookstore," in hindsight a brilliant solution. When Amazon.com expanded its product lines, the tag line changed to "Earth's Biggest Selection"—a choice that accommodated the expanded model of selling much more than books while retaining communication linkage to the Amazon name.

Looks That Matter

Creating a visual identity consists of translating the positioning and verbal identity to a tangible visual representation. The purpose of creating a visual identity is threefold: The first is to bring the brand to life by developing a relevant character and personality to the positioning and name. The second is to aid with the memorability of the brand identity—in other words, to help people remember who you are. The third is to tie all of the disparate brand elements together with the same look and feel. These elements combined make up the core visual identity.

Visual identities are composed of several core elements.

- *The signature:* the brand name in a specific typeface (e.g., the Apple Computer typeface).
- *The logomark:* a graphic element that is realistic or abstract (e.g., the Nike Swoosh).

- *The wordmark:* the brand name treatment as a logo (e.g., Yahoo!).
- *The color:* one or several colors applied to the signature, logomark, or wordmark (e.g., Coca-Cola's red and white).
- *The packaging:* the shapes and materials that play an important role in consumer product identities (e.g., the Absolut bottle).

Consider this common scenario: You walk into a room filled with people you don't know. More than likely, you'll first survey the crowd to look for someone who seems familiar. Next, you may look for someone who is dressed similarly to you or may appear to have a similar background or tastes, or simply looks friendly or approachable. As you introduce yourself and strike up a conversation, you learn the person's name, what she does, where she's from, etc. Within a short period of time you have developed a first impression of this new person, be it positive, negative, or a combination.

In the consumer world, we also gravitate toward the familiar and the comfortable. And we especially gravitate toward something that is relevant to us.

The wine category is a perfect example of this concept. A high percentage of wine purchases are made based upon the design of the label, not intimate knowledge of the winery. When shopping for wines within a certain price range, consumers are often attracted to a label design that they perceive to be of better quality. As an interesting exercise, take a minute to look at a shelf display of wine strictly from a design point-of-view. Then look at the price points of the wines. Does the price match the perceived value created by the design? You will generally not find a $100 Bordeaux in a box. Conversely, a $10 bottle of Chardonnay can turn to cheap chic simply through a unique illustration on the label.

These simple analogies demonstrate how creating an appealing visual identity can balance the overall perception of the brand identity. Whether managing the perceptions of a new brand or changing the perceptions of a repositioned brand, the visual identity elements that you select are crucial in making the positioning and name relevant to your target audience. (This is discussed in more detail in Chapter 4, "The Yin and Yang of Visual Identities.")

The Identity Experience

This last element of the total identity development process is rapidly becoming one of the most important. Regardless of how memorable the name is, how beautiful the design, how much you like advertising, or the price, if you have a negative experience with a brand, that's what you remember. The branded experience is your actual contact with the product or service. It can be the taste, feel, fit, or performance.

Customer service is another experience that can make or break a brand. Was the salesperson friendly or rude? Was the repair technician knowledgeable? Did the waitress forget your order? These concepts are extended to the user interface of Web sites. Was the site easy to navigate and full of useful information? Or was it slow as a slug, overdesigned, and difficult to access?

One of our favorite experience stories involves a well-known software brand. Dave needed to upgrade his software for a project, so he went to the company web site to look for the upgrade. After several minutes, he finally found the appropriate section and proceeded to look for an option to purchase and download the upgrade. The software was only available for order via CD, not as a direct download. In a rush, he ordered and paid extra for next-day delivery. The next day came, but the CD didn't. Well, sometimes mistakes happen.

The number of software outlets catering to Mac users was limited, so there was no choice but to wait. The second day came, but once again the CD didn't. This was now a bona fide strike one. He went back to the site in search of customer support e-mail, but found only FAQs, none of which contained an e-mail address. After scouring the site for a customer service phone number, he finally found a toll-free number buried in an obscure location on the site. By this time 2 days and 3 hours passed.

After spending what seemed like an eternity on hold waiting for customer service, he was told that the overnight delivery was only confirmed after it left the warehouse, not from the order confirmation date. Strike two. Dave told the company's customer service rep that he wished to cancel the order and requested a refund. He was told "no." The product order was in the system and could not be stopped. Because the product was under $100, the company would not accept a return of the CD. (The product was, of course, $99.) However, the rep informed him, the company would issue a refund if the CD was destroyed. After he received the CD, he could call customer service, break it in half while the customer service representative was listening to "confirm destruction," then mail a written request for a refund that would take about 6 weeks for processing. Strike three! Out of curiosity, Dave asked the representative where the warehouse was, and she told him it was less than 30 miles from his house. The CD arrived on the fourth day.

Needless to say, the impact of such an experience can affect one's perceptions, whether most positively or most negatively. And don't forget, every consumer has friends, colleagues, and readers to share these stories with.

Gatorade: Bringing It All Together

Gatorade is a time-honored example of a category leader. Gatorade invented the Thirst Quencher category in 1965 with its product introduction to the University of Florida football team, the Gators. A university research team developed the formula to compensate for severe hydration during workouts and games in the hot, humid Southeast. It was nicknamed "Gatorade" because of the beverage's association with the team's endurance and winning record. In 1967, Stokely–Van Camp purchased the rights to produce and sell the product throughout the United States; this was the birth of a consumer brand. Shortly after acquiring the rights, Stokely signed a licensing agreement with the National Football League, and thus began Gatorade's long association with professional sports. It was later acquired by Quaker Oats and then Pepsico, and it continues to be associated with professional sports as the official sports beverage of the National Football League, National Basketball Association, Major League Baseball, National Hockey

League, and National Association of Stock Car Auto Racing, and a multitude of other sports.

Based on what we covered in our identity ABCs, here's a breakdown of the Gatorade identity:

Positioning

Gatorade is a proprietary formula drink associated with sports. It's always been positioned as a thirst quencher, not an energy drink. The original and current formula was developed to rehydrate and replenish electrolytes—a key feature and benefit. Its core essence is directly associated with sports, performance, and replenishment. Through the years, Gatorade has leveraged its heritage and direct relationship with amateur and professional competitive sports by marketing to teens and "weekend warriors" who seek to enhance their own athletic performance or at the very least be associated with top athletes. Professional athletes and spectators at professional sporting events are other target audiences.

Verbal Identity

The Gatorade name stems from its heritage with the University of Florida Gators football team. The "-ade" ending easily establishes the drink's role as something that aids and assists the athlete. "Thirst Quencher" is a combination of a positioning tag line and a descriptor. Since "Thirst Quencher" is not the everyday, common way to describe the drink, it doesn't qualify as a true generic descriptor. In other words, it was created to be a proprietary mnemonic device the company could own and people would remember. It also uniquely positioned the product in the marketplace. Thanks to its own success and the test of time, "Thirst Quencher" has actually become a descriptor for the entire product category.

Visual Identity

Although there have been several redesigns of the identity and packaging, it is essentially the same product that it was at its inception. David Wisnom led Landor's design team for its 1994 worldwide packaging relaunch in 27 countries. The brand name has always been set in green type in a white rectangular badge (or containment shape) on a field of green. This is reflective of the original color of the lemon-lime flavor. The orange lightening bolt was added to convey the speed and effectiveness of delivery and pays homage to the orange of the University of Florida Gators. Since Gatorade was launched, it has always been in a proprietary package with a wide mouth for speed of delivery. This is a natural extension of its positioning, not unlike the orange Gatorade coolers on the sidelines or "the field of play" at professional sporting events.

Identity Experience

The Gatorade experience means an experience with sports. The brand has been built over time based on its association with professional sports and with athletes such as Michael Jordan. Even if you've never consumed Gatorade, a sporting event has at least been your indirect brand experience. The Gatorade image is based on professional athletes, sports, and performance. Even Sunday hoop players and 16-year-old varsity football players can aspire to greater performance by "drinking what the pros drink." The fact that the product actually delivers its brand promise of quenching thirst makes the product a consistent winner.

2

DEMYSTIFYING
POSITIONING STRATEGY

Strategy, particularly identity positioning strategy, doesn't have to be complicated. It is a roadmap to guide a company in creating a multidimensional identity that can also be the basis for brand-building efforts. Positioning provides the tactical blueprint that anchors the creative vision to then create an identity. It also establishes a plan to consistently manage not only the creation but the implementation and maintenance of the identity by internal brand marketing groups and external creative agencies. While many experts tout a laundry list of strict rules with particular emphasis on creating a brand around knowing a company's audience, we believe an identity strategy should be based on commonsense guidelines that are flexible enough to create much needed maneuvering room for creativity. We also believe identity strategy isn't rocket science.

No Two Strands of DNA Are Alike

The purpose of any strategy is to provide a plan of how to reach a goal. The purpose of an identity strategy is to provide a plan or blueprint of how to verbally and visually communicate a brand's identity relevantly and uniquely to intended audiences. This identity blueprint may be observed as a collective unit or pulled apart as individual components for use in brand-building efforts such as advertising and public relations strategies. It can also be used to create a company, product, or service identity as well as platforms and families of products, services, and technologies. As we discussed in Chapter 1, the components of identity strategy are the proposition, price points, target markets, competitive practices, corporate relationships, target audiences, key features and benefits, audience messaging matrix, communication attributes, core essence, positioning statement, identity objectives, and technical parameters. The strategy is then compared to the building blocks of relativity, personification, assets, and differentiation. Once the strategy is defined it will be used as the basis for all further creative development such as naming, design, copywriting, etc.

The Proposition

The place to start with an identity is reviewing what your company, product, or service actually offers. Referring back to the original business or product plan is the first step in formulating the identity strategy. The type of language and jargon required to fill out a business or product plan is widely known and accepted as a protocol. There is a certain, shall we say, complex lexicon required and expected by the financial investment and analysis community. The ability to take that same information and distill it into a rather layman-like 30-second pitch is the next step to formulating your identity strategy. We call this the *elevator pitch*. You've just stepped onto the elevator and right before the doors close, a principal from a highly coveted venture capital firm walks on and recognizes you. You're asked what's new. You respond with your new company/product/service. Keep in mind the person has to step off in three floors for an urgent meeting. What do you say? Can you articulate the proposition by the time the person exits and feel confident that he "got it" in 30 to 60 seconds? Does it take you 5 to 10 minutes to explain the new venture, or can you distill the basic information to less than a minute? This is an excellent exercise to actually try out with your team to test the proposition for brevity.

In addition to time, the other crucial part of the proposition pitch is using language that is as jargon-free as possible. In other words, can you explain your new company/product/service in words that even your Great Aunt Milly in Tacoma would understand? Another exercise we use to test the language is aptly titled "talk to a 4-year-old." As many of you know, 4-year-olds are quite inquisitive, wanting to know how things work and why things are the way they are. They also have relatively short attention spans. You're now explaining your proposition to your 4-year-old niece, Anna. Anna wants to know more about your work. You have less than a minute to explain it to her. Go!

"Well, Anna, we create PMEs based on XML for WANs, empowering wireless telecoms to manage and deliver Web-based data via PCs, mobile phones, wireless PDAs, and TV set-top boxes."

Is a 4-year-old really going to understand this?

"Well, Anna, we create software that makes it easier for companies to send information to people on things that don't require wires, like cell phones and computers you can carry with you."

Yes, Anna would approve. We have gone through this exercise many a time with clients, and inevitably there are those who truly become stuck on simplifying language to this degree. It becomes a challenge because it's perceived as not smart or clever language. Inevitably, we always remind people that when all is said and done, this is the basic message for what the new offering is all about. Stripping it down to this level allows the essential message to emerge. Crafting it to sound more melodious and perhaps even sophisticated occurs after this point. Think of the basic framework of a house. Custom-crafted siding doesn't go on until the structure is in place.

"Well, Anna, we deliver infrastructure software for the wireless telecommunications industry, allowing wireless carriers to manage and deliver Web-based information in multiple languages across all data-enabled devices."

This basic statement is recrafted for its actual audiences with a bit more sophistication. It doesn't rely heavily on jargon, so it doesn't lose its clarity.

From $ to Dollars

Knowing your price points for products and services is of particular importance to people concerned with sales, revenues, profits, and margins. Truth be known, the details of the numbers are not nearly as important to identity people as they are to financial analysts. Where it is important to the identity is in establishing the price point as an attribute. Pricing can create a perception of value. Words like "premium," "value," "midtier" and "cost-effective" are used and often abused to create an association between the numeric and the linguistic. We say abused because these words are so pervasive that they demand further clarification to be unique, ownable, and defensible.

In order to further clarify and assign richer meaning, we often use brand associations in commonly understood categories, such as cars or clothing. Take the word "premium," for example. If your new biotech product is to be offered at a premium price tier, experiment with widely recognized brand associations to further define what exactly is meant by "premium." Is it premium like Lexus? Or premium like Porsche? Is it premium like the Porsche Boxster or the Porsche Carrera? Is it premium like the Porsche Carrera or premium like Ferrari Testerosá and so on? These real-world brand analogies help to define where the company/product/service lives in the premium (or midtier or cost-effective) spectrum and therefore sets the stage for an appropriate verbal and visual tone.

The Market Factors

Listing actual or intended geographical sales markets (both short- and long-term) are the next section to identify. Knowing the intended geographic reach is important from an identity perspective for two reasons: (1) It can translate to the positioning, and (2) there may be cultural and linguistic issues.

Let's take how it can translate to positioning. Consider the two brands J. Crew and Agnes B. Both are companies that offer clothing ranging from casual to office wear for both women and men. In the price spectrum, J. Crew costs more than something purchased at the Gap. Agnes B. is more expensive than J. Crew and costs roughly the same as Emporio Armani, Giorgio Armani's ready-to-wear brand. Neither are considered couture nor designer wear, nor are they considered cheap chic. Both carry initialized personal names aimed roughly at the same age range. Both have signature stores from Union Square in San Francisco to Tokyo. Both can be considered part of the global market. The difference in positioning comes from leveraging their market origination. Based in New York City, J. Crew is distinctly all-American and boasts an identity and image that leverages it. Agnes B. is distinctly French chic and specifically Parisian. The visual identities, the clothing itself, and the retail environments reflect each of their intended nationalities. These are beautiful examples of two similar brands using their market origins as attributes of their brand personalities, and therefore of differentiation.

The second reason markets are important to an identity is because of cultural and linguistic concerns. If a company, product, or service markets itself to countries outside the United States, cultural and linguistic appropriateness of the identity are needed to fit in with the customs and language. "Fitting in" in this sense simply means not offending or evoking incredulous laughter from the native population. The Chevrolet Nova story is the textbook case for what happens when cultural and linguistic appropriateness is ignored. The Nova was named for the celestial (star) phenomenon and was introduced with great success in the United States. When Chevrolet hoped for a repeated success in Mexico, the company was a bit chagrined to learn that it was marketing a car whose name translated to "doesn't go" in Spanish. This classic tale of international ignorance is actually an urban legend. Apparently sales in Spanish-language markets were not significantly affected by the Nova name, as the tale claims. What may be myth for GM and the Nova was true-to-life for Japanese car maker Mitsubishi. The Mitsubishi Montero was first christened the Pajero—which turns out to be Spanish slang for someone who enjoys pleasuring himself. Oops. Fact or fiction, these are extremely good cautionary tales of what can go wrong when executives don't do their research in foreign markets.

Including your intended markets (both short- and long-term) in the identity strategy will set the stage for what we call the *technical parameters* of naming and design. They also serve as a reminder of what markets and languages should be checked in order to avoid any potential embarrassments. (For more on cultural and linguistic appropriateness, see Chapter 3, "The Anomaly of Naming.")

Target Audiences

Knowing who your target audience is, is as important to an identity as it is for a sales strategy. The common denominator is identifying whom you're selling to, and how and why. The more you know about your target customer, and can see and hear with *their* eyes and ears, the more relevantly you can communicate to them about your company, product, or service.

We break down the concept into primary and secondary audiences. The *primary audience* includes those industries, companies, and individuals that most closely match the intended demographic profile and positioning. For example, Gatorade's primary target audience in the early 1990s was 12- to 18-year-olds who intensely engage in competitive sports. A brand's *secondary audience* consists of those farther from the core demographics who still may buy the product or service. The secondary audience for Gatorade was adult weekend warriors—guys shooting hoops on a Sunday wanting to live in the fantasy of their glory days in sports. Secondary audiences may also be individuals or entities who influence the presentation of the brand: for example, employees, financial analysts, advisory boards, journalists. They can also be purchasers who are not the main target. Hence, the nature of being secondary. This leads us to the distinction between purchasers and influencers.

It's important to understand the distinction between purchasers and influencers when identifying potential customers for products and services. Consider kids' cereal: Is the primary audience kids who eat the cereal or moms who purchase the cereal? Kids influence their moms by asking for the item, but moms actually purchase the cereal. Distinguishing between the purchaser and the influencer allows us to create balance in the positioning and messaging—in this case, appealing to kids but obviously not alienating moms.

Let's take another example: business software. You're trying to sell marketing management software to an online consumer products company. The primary audience is the marketing department, and the secondary audience is the information technology department, correct? Look more closely. The actual users of the software are members of the marketing team. The IT department comes in because the software resides on the internal network and must be able to integrate with the Web site's servers and access data to mine key information. In addition, a system administrator needs to be trained to maintain the system within the IT department. The software costs $1 million; hence, this brings the finance department into the fold not only because of the purchase price but also because of the ongoing maintenance, support, and training expenses. So who is the purchaser and who is the influencer?

The marketing department is a primary audience because it is a primary user and beneficiary. However, because of the significant cost and involvement of the IT department, the vice president of marketing is only one of many influencers of the purchase. The IT department needs to determine the product's viability, ease of integration, and ongoing maintenance. Therefore, the chief technical officer (CTO) influences the purchase as well. Due to the significant upfront costs and training and maintenance expenses, the chief financial officer (CFO) makes the final decision to purchase the software based on increased productivity and return on investment (ROI).

Distinguishing between primary and secondary audiences, and purchasers and influencers, can make a world of difference when it comes to creating the messaging to each group. Using defined and prioritized audiences as a tool for creating messaging is discussed at length later in this chapter and in Chapter 5, "Identity Messaging."

Knowing the Competition

In completing your business or product plan, you learn about other companies trying to sell similar products or services to a similar set of people—if not the exact same ones. Remember that from an identity perspective indirect competitors are as important as direct competitors, if for no other reason than to avoid the me-too syndrome. In addition to the "what/where/how/to whom" profile of each entity in your marketplace, it's highly beneficial to conduct a verbal and visual analysis of their identities. What does their logo look like? What colors and shapes are used? Do they only use a wordmark? What is their name? Do they use a descriptor or positioning tag line or both? If so, what are they? How do they describe what they do on their web site or brochure? How are they unique? How are they the same? Retaining a research firm to conduct brand awareness/recognition or brand asset studies based on defined customer segments can provide more detailed information. Whether you use formal research as a guide or conduct informal verbal and visual identity audits, the ability to refer back to what each competitor says, looks like, and acts like is key to noting how distinct or alike each identity is.

For instance, there may be certain visual practices a majority of competitors use, such as the color blue as a wordmark. This will serve as a warning flag of what to avoid. When the time comes to create a visual identity, select another dominant color, such as red or green, with a logo in addition to a typographic treatment. Adopting a blue wordmark like everyone else reduces the amount of differentiation the total identity can enjoy. On the other hand, identifying common language practices is extremely helpful in assessing what words are industry-pervasive and accepted and where there is room for creating differentiated messaging.

Corporate Relationships

We define a corporate relationship as the relationship of the company or holding company to the entity that is to be branded. The relationship must be defined in order to leverage or minimize either brand. If the new brand is a new *product* or *service* (or platform of products and services), then the strategy, name, and visual identity should either leverage or minimize the company brand's equity. If it is a new *company* brand, with a parent company brand already in existence, then once again the strategy, name, and visual identity should either leverage or minimize the parent's brand equity. Why leverage or minimize? Depending on the existing brand strengths, including loyalty and recognition, there may be a strong case to leverage and closely mimic the existing brand. A new brand from Microsoft, for instance, has a far better chance of obtaining instant product brand recognition based on the Microsoft company brand recognition than the new product brand by itself. On the other hand, the parent brand may have some significant weaknesses that need to be downplayed or avoided. Weaknesses can range from credibility to financial integrity to simply being in an industry that is too far removed from the new marketplace—such as a financial services company launching an online dating service. Another time to minimize the parent brand, or even omit it altogether, is when a new product is offered at an extremely low price point but the brand has traditionally been known for premium products—or vice versa.

Determining the relationship sets the stage for choosing a brand model. This is sometimes also referred to as *brand nomenclature* or an *architecture model.* Choosing a brand model can occur at any point in the strategy and often comes in the form of strategy recommendations from agencies and consultants. There are four basic models to choose from: dominant, equal, subordinate, invisible.

Corporate Dominant

In the dominant model, the corporate brand is the thread for all marketing activities. All divisions, products, and services carry the corporate brand with a generically descriptive modifier that uses common language instead of proprietary language or names to communicate the intended product or service. Few additional brands exist outside this model. For example, Yahoo! uses its corporate brand name to brand most of its services, such as Yahoo! Yellow Pages, Yahoo! Auctions, Yahoo! E-mail. The corporate name is used in conjunction with generic descriptors to create a service name. Occasionally, the corporate brand can be extended in a proprietary way such as with Yahooligans or Yahoo's Kids' Directory.

The huge advantage to this model is that emphasis is placed wholly on the company, rather than attention being divided among competing proprietary brand names. The other advantage is cost-effectiveness. In this model, there is only one trademark to worry about as the product or service names are created with generic descriptors. For newer or smaller companies with limited budgets, the corporate dominant model is an excellent strategy to employ.

Equal Brands

While the corporate dominant strategy relies on generic language to create product and service names, the equal brand model relies on creating new proprietary brand names that are accompanied by the company brand name. Equal brands mean that a company name and new product or service brand name get equal time both verbally and visually. Examples include AT&T WorldNet, Microsoft Word, or in the case of one of Yahoo's naming exceptions, Yahoo! PayDirect.

This model is clearly more costly to create and maintain, but the reward is multiple brands that can strengthen the corporate brand both perceptually and financially. Brands come and go. Some can be highly successful, and others real stinkers. The company brand can benefit from this waxing and waning by selling the brand to another company (such as Xerox ContentGuard, now known as ContentGuard) or by allowing one brand's success to make up for some losses. The model can also give the perception of a greater breadth of differentiated products and services.

Corporate Subordinate

The corporate subordinate model is the reverse of the dominant model (see Figure 2–1). The new product or service name appears as the dominant marketing emphasis, while the corporate brand is secondary.

Corprorate Dominant

NewCorp, Inc.

Corprorate Equal

NewCorp NewBrand

Corprorate Subordinate

NewBrand
A Division of NewCorp, Inc.

Corprorate Invisible

NewBrand

Figure 2–1. Corporate branding models.

This subordinate relationship can be established verbally—for example, Alpha by Newco or Alpha from
Newco—or visually with a visible but proportionately
smaller visual treatment of the corporate brand. In
the case of a parent or holding company, a *strap line,*
or legal identifier, can be created verbally and visually
to establish a relationship: for example, HBO, A Division of Time Warner Entertainment, L.P. This strap
line can be a permanent verbal and visual element of
the total identity, or it can be used selectively, such as
for legal and corporate activity purposes.

The subordinate model is advantageous for two
main reasons. In the case of a new brand created from
scratch, endorsement via the parent brand lends credibility and instant recognition. Again refer to our ear-

lier Microsoft example. The second reason is that it can enhance the parent's company status, especially in the financial world. The image perceived is large, substantial, and value-rich. The strap line is also helpful in establishing credibility and recognition for a new company brand, for example, Newco, a GE Company.

Corporate Invisible

In the corporate invisible model, the relationship between the corporate and product or service brand is not apparent to end users and is limited to corporate, legal, and financial activities. All divisions and products maintain their own brand identities, with no linkage to the corporate brand or to one another. Classic examples of the corporate invisible model are Procter & Gamble and Sara Lee.

This model can be distinctly advantageous when one company holds one or many brands that either fall outside the company's main scope: for example, a health service company that owns a toy store chain. It's also advantageous when cross-marketing and selling. For instance, AOL Time Warner can market music from the latest teen pop singer signed to Warner Music by placing the music in Dawson's Creek, a teen show on the WB station, and promoting the CD on

HBO to Time Kids to AOL. The average consumer is generally not aware that all products and channels are owned by the same parent company. The obvious down side is that creating, implementing, and maintaining this model takes the most financial and human resources, time, and commitment.

Key Features and Benefits

Identifying common language practices in a given industry or marketplace is the basis of effective features and benefits. Features and benefits can be both tangible and intangible. Features are the tangible elements offered to a customer: ingredients, serving size, hours of operation, number of offices, etc. Features can be functional, proprietary, differentiated, or industry standard. Examples include:

- Spill-proof top
- 800 number for customer service
- Global corporation with 500 offices
- Real-time, diagnostic control panel

Benefits can be either tangible or intangible. Every feature has a benefit, and in some cases, more than one.

- Faster processing speed
- Flexibility

- Convenience
- Relieves pain faster

Features and benefits should be gleaned from a business or product plan, the research and development department, the engineering department, the marketing department, or a combination of the above. The point is to gather from all available resources an exhaustive list of features and corresponding benefits. Rewriting the lists into clear, easy-to-understand language is crucial as each department will have its own style for describing benefits. When rewriting, refer back to your target audiences and findings from competitive audits. Will the audience understand the feature or benefit in a few seconds? Is the list written in language widely understood in the industry—or is it jargon-heavy? Once rewritten for clarity and relevancy, create a two-column list: features on the left-hand side, corresponding benefits on the right.

Once the list is complete, the task of prioritizing features and benefits begins. While nearly all can be used in copy for, say, a sales sheet, a list of the top 10 or even top 5 features and corresponding benefits is required for the fundamental identity strategy. At this point we recommend comparing and reviewing features and benefits with your competitive information once again to assess what is industry standard and what is truly unique and differentiated within the industry. In prioritizing the final list, bump up the differentiated features and benefits to the top of the list. The last thing you want is the first 5 out of 10 features and benefits to be industry commodities. Make sure some differentiated features and benefits are in the top 5 list. If you find you have absolutely no unique features and benefits, we suggest going back to the business model drawing board. We don't mean this facetiously. We've actually experienced this scenario with a couple of former clients. After going through the positioning strategy process, they realized the basic service model needed to be reviewed and restructured before they could proceed with identity creation and brand building.

Keep in mind that the order of the features and benefits will change according to your target audience. What is most important to the IT director may be very unimportant to the CFO. This is also true of the needs of the 8-year-old boy and that of his mother. Prioritizing features and benefits according to target audiences is the essence of the audience messaging matrix. With this said, it's equally important to establish the initial list that is the common thread regardless of individual audiences. Think of it as the color palette to choose from, depending on the artistic application.

Audience Messaging Matrix

The audience messaging matrix is a marvelous tool based upon the concept of hierarchy of communication. Hierarchy of communication is the theory of presenting key information in the order most relevant to the target audiences. Imagine being at the grocery store looking for a fruit-flavored diet soft drink. You may be scanning shelves filled with nearly 100 choices of different brands, different flavors, low-calorie, regular, caffeine-free, cans versus bottles, different bottle sizes and pack configurations, etc. If you have a favorite brand, you generally look for the brand first, then flavor, then low-calories. If you don't have a brand preference, you will look for the flavor first then confirm that it's low-calorie. You select the product based upon what information is most relevant to you. In positioning a new company, product, or service, it's essential to understand what is relevant to each target audience through qualitative research. This way you can establish a ranking order of your brand's features and benefits and positioning, according to each audience segment. Therefore, brand communication is more relevant to each individual audience, and the consumer or prospect "gets it" faster. The audience messaging matrix is very helpful to establishing messaging in marketing and sales collateral, web sites, etc. We discuss examples and applying the audience messaging matrix to messaging in Chapter 5.

Communication Attributes

Communication attributes are a list of adjectives that suggest descriptively, figuratively, or evocatively what the brand is like. These attributes are associational and provide definition of the brand as a personality. They are those qualities and traits that you describe to your friend about the girl or guy of your dreams— presented always in the best light and perhaps with a bit of aspiration. Communication attributes are used as a palette of words—the rudimentary colors that bring the total brand identity to life. These attributes are the focal point for all creative development, be it naming, messaging, visual identity design, web and print design, and even copywriting.

In order for a brand identity to be successful, it must go beyond the static or even the theoretical and be developed as a fully dimensional persona. If full dimensionality is the desired outcome, then developing the typical stale list of attributes is something to avoid at all cost. How many times have you heard the following adjectives: premier, leading, innovative, cutting edge, reliable, global, premium? These are dull, flat, overused words that tend to be used together. They're communication commodities. They sound safe. Everyone uses them, so why not us?

It was through our own experiences, and particularly Alycia's naming experiences, that we identified this disturbing trend, which we ourselves had indeed been a part of. It seemed that every creative brief written to direct the creative development of names had the exact same list of communication attributes—and therefore communication commodities. As they say, garbage in, garbage out. Consequently, far too many lists of names created were the same for every company. Think of the average individual: Would you say that describing your best friend Joe Jones as tall, dark, and average looking is a complete picture of who he is? What if I described Joe Jones this way: dark curly hair, blue eyes, 6'2", thin build, technical writer, lives in a loft in the Mission district of San Francisco, drives a brand-new silver Z3, gives regularly to the local homeless shelter, and hires a cleaner once a week to clean up his mess? Suddenly Joe's profile becomes more dimensional and tangible. More life, therefore more tangibility.

So how do you create this list? In the past, we have conducted creative workshops to break people out of the static mindset and into broader thinking. Techniques include everything from writing and drawing exercises to musical improvisation. Tapping into other senses such as sight and sound and doing unexpected things like using crayons in a corporate office to draw what your brand looks helps your mind to step outside the vernacular. Using creative techniques that are simple and evocative and build upon each other truly makes the difference between a breakthrough and the blahs. We always recommend an objective facilitator in these sessions, especially when it comes time for consensus building and narrowing the list down. In our own sessions, we have had as many as 100 attributes listed. An identity strategy needs no more than 10. Narrowing down the list is a process of comparison and elimination. What are the obvious attributes to eliminate? When words start to overlap in meaning, such as "streamlined" and "efficient" or "transparent" and "invisible," compare the sets and choose based on nuance. Paying attention to the subtleties of words is crucial—each nuance can indeed speak volumes about the brand. Is our product more streamlined or is it more efficient? Is the technology transparent or invisible? Is the food product ubiquitous or widely available? What is it now? What does it aspire to be 18 months from now? Thinking ahead (whether that's 18 technology months or the traditional 5 to 6 years of a product cycle) will allow the brand to grow into itself. It's kind of like buying clothes for a kid—always choose the next size up in case he can't fit into them by next week.

Core Essence

Once the top 10 communication attributes are established, the core essence of the identity can be established. The core essence is defined as the intrinsic and indispensable properties that characterize the brand. The core essence defines what your brand stands for in one to two words. What is your brand about? Is it about empowerment, pleasure, magic, performance, simplified communication? How does your essence relate to the positioning of your key competitors? Is it differentiated or just another flavor? The core essence identified should be or become your brand's main strength. It's what makes you more relevant and differentiated.

For example, cellular phone companies are all about wireless communication. They are commodities offering the same basic service. However, some are positioned as the cheapest, some as the clearest, some offer the best or broadest coverage, and others the most value. Each of the positions is an attempt to differentiate via a real or perceived strength. The more clear and simple the core essence, the more clear and simple the communication, the more quickly the prospective customer will understand what is intended.

Positioning Statement

If the core essence is a one- or two-word impression of the brand, the positioning statement is the definitive source of what the brand and offer is all about. Time is critical and the need to know within seconds is often the norm. That's what makes a positioning statement the center point of strategy. A positioning statement is one to two sentences that clearly and succinctly articulate the company, product, or service definition, its key features, and its benefits or USPs (unique selling propositions), target audiences, markets, and relevant corporate relationships: parent company, subsidiary relationship, etc. The statement is both factual and evocative and uses communication attributes as relevant adjectives.

A well-crafted positioning statement should communicate within 30 seconds what the company, product, or service is for and why it's relevant to anyone— from the company's administrative assistant to your neighbor next door. While we state that a positioning statement is for general audiences, alternative statements with a different hierarchy of communication may also be crafted for specific audiences, such as the investment community or vertical markets. Here is the most rudimentary structure of a positioning statement:

A (company/product/service) is a B (definition) that provides C (benefit) to D (target audiences) in E (markets).

When using a two-sentence statement, write the second sentence to call out USPs and/or proprietary technologies, patents, and other top-level benefits. Remember, communication attributes are merely adjectives of the identity. Use them accordingly throughout the statement. Here is a handy template:

A (company/product/service) is a B (definition) that provides C (benefit) to D (target audiences) in E (markets). F (USP, proprietary technology, patent) provides G (new benefit) and H (new benefit or other top-level information).

The following is an example from one of our past technology clients who required a new company name. Newco is the placeholder name.

Newco provides software infrastructure essential for the wireless information industry worldwide. Through its unique XML-based open technology,

Newco specializes in adaptive, integral solutions that personalize and simplify presentation and content distribution to data-enabled devices, regardless of platform or language.

Identity Objectives and Technical Parameters

The final components of the strategy relate directly to the verbal and visual creative development such as naming and design objectives. They are the goals and guidelines around which to name and design a brand. The technical parameters are the practical and functional aspects that govern creative development, such as markets and languages to be aware of, verbal and visual relationships to the corporate brand (brand model), specific creative directions to avoid, and so on. Objectives and technical parameters are covered in more depth in the next chapters.

Back to Relativity

Once the strategy is at an initial stage of completion, run the individual components through our brand relativity equation:

Brand relativity = relevance + personification
+ assets + differentiation

How relevant are the strategy components to the intended audiences? How multidimensional is the identity personality? Have you leveraged your existing brand assets appropriately? What assets are missing? Have you strengthened or minimized your weaknesses? And finally is the strategic structure of your identity unique and distinctive, or do you appear as another me-too? Measuring the strategy against the brand relativity equation through qualitative and quantitative research is an excellent validation and guidance tool.

We stated earlier that positioning strategy isn't rocket science. It does, however, require diligence to flesh out all components. While this can be done entirely in-house, a freelance consultant or identity agency can bring objectivity and a fresh, unbiased set of eyes and ears to the task, helping to ensure that the strategy is unique, ownable, and defensible. Once you've made it to this point, congratulations! The identity is ready to come to life.

3

THE ANOMALY
OF NAMING

For the longest time, naming had a bad rap as a practice. Even in the early 1990s when Alycia first became a dedicated naming consultant, it was difficult to convince managers and executives to realize the value of hiring outside consultants to name a company or, God forbid, a product, service, or line extension. Typical responses ranged from "What? Couldn't we come up with something over a pizza and beer?" to "I named my kid. I named my dog. How hard could it be?"

The Evolution of Names

Eponymous Who?

Once upon a time, it was simple. An artisan signed his work. A merchant hung out a shingle with his name on it. Whether it was hard goods, consumables, or financial services being offered, it didn't matter—the person represented the brand. The name on the door was a declaration that this was the best product, the best service, and the maker would stake his reputation on it.* In the naming world, these personal names turned brand names are known as *eponymous names.* Caswell & Massey, John Deere, Charles Schwab are just a few examples. In the case of fashion, designers' names such as Gucci, Georgio Armani, and Christian Dior are a testament of the best taste and style.

Descriptive Language

With the advent of the industrial age and large corporations, the need to appear trustworthy and intimate

---

*At the time, women were rarely found in the upper echelons of business. The notable exception is Madame C.J. Walker, a former washerwoman born in 1867 who became the first self-made female millionaire in the United States.

gave way to the desire to appear—for lack of better words—large. The eponymous companies of the nineteenth century Edison General Electric and Bell Telephone became the twenty-first-century corporate behemoths GE and AT&T. In the period between, descriptive names suggesting a ubiquitous presence were adopted, expanding the perception of a smaller company (i.e., a one-person shop) to the large corporation. General Electric (from the merger of Edison General Electric Company and Thomson-Houston Company), American Telephone & Telegraph, and later in the twentieth century International Business Machines (originally called Computing-Tabulating-Recording Company, named from the previous mergers and acquisitions of International Time Recording Company, Computing Scale Company of America, and Tabulating Machine Company) are just a few examples. Each of these names worked very well for many years and accurately described the core offer of each company.

Acronym Soup

Eventually each of these brands ran into the same problem: they grew beyond that core offer. As we've all come to know, technologies come and go, and what's hot today can be next year's Ford Pinto. Still think of AT&T as offering telegraph services or exclusively American? How about IBM as business machines? It all sounds a bit silly by today's standards and technologies. Again, appropriate meanings then, but not even close now. What's even sillier is saying a mouthful like "International Business Machines." Go ahead—try saying that quickly three times. After years of building brand equity, these companies made the wise choice: they simply abbreviated the descriptive names into acronyms.

AT&T, IBM, GE—even Kentucky Fried Chicken changed to KFC in the 1990s on the recommendation of Landor Associates. A backlash against acronyms began, however, in the mid-1980s as the high-tech sector overused the practice, creating a virtual alphabet soup. As more and more companies abbreviated their names, and high-tech companies created more programming languages, protocols, platforms, products, and services (most sporting descriptive names turned acronym), acronyms became increasingly generic. CD-ROM (compact disk–read-only memory), DOS (disk operating system), HTML (hypertext markup language), CPU (central processing unit), ISP (Internet service provider), and ASP (application service provider) are just a few most of us remember as acronyms only.

Figurative and Evocative Names

One of the next naming methods followed the trend that Procter & Gamble and Unilever made famous roughly a century earlier: creating figurative and evocative names. Ivory's name is reputed to have been inspired by the Forty-fifth Psalm: "All thy garments smell of myrrh and aloes and cassia, out of ivory palaces whereby they have made thee glad." This tied in beautifully with the soap's white and pure USP (unique selling proposition) and famous tag line, "99 and 44/100 percent pure.[1] Ivory: the word itself evokes beautiful, pure, white, strong—all the key communication attributes the product offered. These attributes, together with feminine, gentle-looking packaging, conveyed its key benefit communication of "gentle but clean." Just think of all that communication stemming from a single word. This was the appeal of evocative names: visceral communication combined with brevity. Dove, Sunlight, Fab, Sprite, Bounce, Crest, Squirt, Dash, Tide—all appeal to the senses in a highly concise way.

While figurative and evocative names filled the grocery and five-and-dime store shelves, they were rarely connected with company or service names. The names of the companies that birthed these products were themselves mostly eponymous: Procter &

Gamble, Colgate-Palmolive, Unilever. These two-handled names were also often eponymous in origin: Unilever derives from the 1930 merger of the Dutch margarine company Margarine Unie and the British soapmaker Lever Brothers, founded by William Hesketh Lever in 1885.[2]

The Palmolive half of Colgate-Palmolive may have been one of the original success stories of transferring an evocative product name to a company name. In 1898, when B. J. Johnson Soap Company introduced Palmolive, which descriptively communicated the unique ingredients of palm and olive oils in the soap, the product and the name were a smashing success—so much so that the company changed its name to Palmolive in 1916 and eventually merged with Colgate to form Colgate-Palmolive.[3]

Real-Word Names

Real-word names are just that—words that exist in a living language that are applied as a name. (We could say this extends to dead languages as well, but let's be honest, would you really know what *apricus* means if we didn't tell you it's "to bask in the sun" in Latin?) You've already heard the term figurative referred to above. Simply put, it is a literal word for a person, place, or thing.

Cast your mind back a couple of decades. When Steve Jobs and Steve Wozniak were first trying to come up with a name for their new company, IBM was king. Imagine sitting in a room of colleagues and investors waiting anxiously to hear the name of the company that is about to revolutionize the micro-computer world. And we are proud to present . . . Apple! Long, pregnant pause. We did just say revolutionize the microcomputer world in a time when IBM was king, right? Apple? Apple brand body lotion maybe, but Apple Computer Company?

Well, in truth, this is not the real history of Apple's birth. According to the official version, Jobs

Figure 3–1. Apple's original corporate identity.

and Wozniak pooled their financial resources together, and on April 1, 1976, they formed the Apple Computer Company. Jobs had recently worked at an organic apple orchard and liked the name. "He thought of the apple as the perfect fruit—it has a high nutritional content, it comes in a nice package, it doesn't damage easily—and he wanted Apple to be the perfect company. Besides, they couldn't come up with a better name."[4]

You have to admit, it took prescience and guts to go with that name. It was and is the quintessential example of a real word, a figurative name, applied to a company that worked. Today this strategy is still highly effective when used in unexpected contexts, for example, Orange (telecom) or Oxygen (television channel).

Portmanteaus

Portmanteau is a French word meaning a large leather suitcase that opens into two hinged compartments. In the naming world, it's a fancy way of saying two words or word parts smooshed together to form a new word. The prefix "micro," meaning small, and "soft," from software, together make Microsoft—software for the microcomputer.

Portmanteau names (such as Microsoft, Content-Guard, WorldNet, Costco) are often constructed from descriptive words. Portmanteaus are useful ways to communicate the core business offer, feature, benefit, geographical span, or origin in a straightforward manner and also retain proprietary distinction. Thus, they can be registered as trademarks. They have the potential to be inventive and highly communicative. It's little wonder that portmanteau names continue to be so popular.

Ironically, by today's standards, the famous Microsoft name falls flat. When constructing names, it's critical to have as the base the company's (or product's or service's) communication attributes. As we discussed in Chapter 2, the communication attributes become the conceptual palette from which to create verbal and visual constructs. The strongest (i.e., most relevant and differentiated) attributes are the ones typically applied to the name.

Keep in mind that a name is generally only a word or two and therefore can communicate only so many things. A list of 10 communication attributes, no matter how smashing and distinctive, will not be conveyed in one to two words. It's remarkable if a name can communicate two to three attributes at a time. Again, a name is a word—not a magical cureall.

In the case of Microsoft, the attributes employed and communicated are "software for the microcomputer," but this core communication leaves us wanting a bit more. We don't mean that Microsoft is a terrible name in and of itself, merely that by today's standards of name creation, this highly descriptive relevant approach would lack uniqueness and differentiation from others in the same marketplace. In 2001, Microsoft was ranked as the second most valuable brand in the world by Interbrand and Business Week.[5] This is a result of (1) being early to market, (2) having lots of time, and (3) having lots of money. It's amazing what these three things can do together.

Many companies and venture capitalists in the early days of the Internet earnestly believed that start-ups could capture the same amount of mind share as, say, a Microsoft or Lucent simply by thinking up an ultra-hip name and, more importantly, by being early to market. We can't tell you how many start-up clients we had during this period who wanted a name like Lucent Technologies. They forgot that Lucent enjoyed a few other key ingredients: AT&T heritage, lots of money . . . and lots of money. Yes, they did have a bit more time, too—all of 4 years prior to the Internet boom. It seems absurd now, but in Internet time those precious 4 years were the equivalent of decades.

Another interesting example of a portmanteau is FedEx. Originally named Federal Express, the express transportation company eventually faced some name communication issues as it sought to provide international service. "Federal" in and of itself had a limiting context for a company that provided a global service. In Spanish-speaking countries the term "Federal" translated to "Federale" and the *federales* (police) were not looked upon kindly. Through extensive research and equity studies with Landor, the company decided on a course of action to change the name to what consumers were already calling it: FedEx. Like so many names before it, the brand name had morphed into a verb: "I'm going to FedEx the package to Cleveland." Rather than risk losing such a valuable asset to generic use (think xerox, aspirin, thermos, and elevator), the company shortened its name to leverage the asset, maximize visual space on white delivery trucks, and get rid of the confining communication and cultural-linguistic problems. Since 2000, the parent company (formerly FDX Corp.) has adopted the powerful FedEx brand name and extended the name to all of its holdings, creating an extremely strong and clear nomenclature based on the FedEx brand name.

Coined Words

When George Eastman first started his photography company, he chose the eponymous route, but as the company expanded, and particularly with the development of simple one-button cameras that could be put into the hands of millions, he felt that a new name was required. According to Kodak history, Eastman began playing around with letters and arbitrarily came up with the word "Kodak." He simply liked the way K's sounded.[6] In fact, Eastman was on to something. Of all the letters in the alphabet, K is one of the most distinctive because it is only rarely used at the beginning of words in the English language. Unlike Q, another distinctive letter, K was also quite easy to pronounce and pleasant to say. So it came to be that the bookends of K—K became the framework for building a new name. From there on it was a matter of filling in the blank with something equally easy to pronounce and pleasant to say. Kodak was born. What's the catch? It's in the phonetics. What's the meaning? There isn't any. It is what we naming consultants call a meaningless name.

Hence, one of the first modern occurrences of a coined or made-up name was an exercise in Scrabble, so to speak. Häagen-Dazs ice cream, for example, is not some Scandinavian-sounding delicacy, but actually an all-American brand started by an entrepreneur from the Bronx and now owned by the Pillsbury Company. Although coined names that are meaningless still exist, it's usually significantly harder to launch a name without inherent meaning and gain traction in today's market because of the sheer number of brand names it must compete with for consumer awareness.

Coined names are still highly desirable especially when creating an international name that will truly "live" in other cultures and markets. While there's no question that English is the *lingua franca* of the day, there are times when real English words or even word parts are not culturally or linguistically appropriate. (More on cultural and linguistic appropriateness for international naming later in this chapter.) There may be the desire to appear as an international entity and/or one with much more stature and credibility, versus a strictly American, young, trendy company. This is when coined names can be very useful.

Other than meaningless coined names, one can create a name out of prefixes, phonemes and suffixes based on living or even dead languages. In other words, we must approach word creation in a similar manner to that of a linguist. The big difference is that brand names may not always make sense linguistically speaking. While the advantage to creating a name out of a living language is obvious, why in the world would one want to create one from a dead language? Latin (a much more popular choice than, say, Aramaic) is the root of many Indo-European languages, including our own. Choosing a Latin-based name has the potential to translate (either literally or loosely) into a broader range of languages. When Philip Morris needed to reinvent its overall identity, it arrived at the new name Altria. The name is derived from *altus,* Latin for "high," suggesting high stature in a soft, fluid, even feminine way. We say feminine because of the use of open vowels (names with hard consonants—for example, Altex—sound more masculine). Further, by virtue of being based on a classical language, the name suggests sophistication, maturity, and stature.

A coined English-based name has its merits: there is a wide choice of words and, perhaps more important, a wide range of tones available. The tone of the name can range from highly descriptive, such as Informix, to highly irreverent, such as FogDog. Here are some common tones.

- *Meaningless:* has no inherent meaning (Kodak).
- *Descriptive:* describes a company, product, service, or target audience. (ContentGuard) or the benefits and features of same (*Real Simple* magazine).

- *Figurative:* a color, thing, place (Oxygen television).
- *Irreverent:* pushes the envelope, uses a tongue-in-cheek description (Pete's Wicked Ale).
- *Emotional:* evokes human emotion (Excite).
- *Personal:* evokes ownership, intimacy (My Yahoo!).

The Naming Process

For some reason naming simultaneously revs the creative juices and instills terror in managers. Naming a company, product, or service seems like a fun project. It's not another boring project report; rather, it's a task where managers can give free rein to their imaginations. Some managers prefer to navigate the creative waters alone. Others enlist a few project members or call on their wives and kids. Still others bring the entire company into the naming process as a way to build company camaraderie. Most start the process with a blank piece of paper and call upon the muses for inspiration, perhaps with a libation or two to Dionysus for good measure.

Now if this process actually worked well, there wouldn't be dozens of independent naming agencies and countless naming consultants and divisions.

Naming is much more than employees creating cool names over a pizza and beer. Legal and Internet domain issues, cultural and linguistic appropriateness, translation ability, memorability, pronunciation, and even spelling all contribute to the complexity of naming. There's also the issue of what the name actually communicates about the company and how it is extended to products, services, and technologies.

The simple reason for these added complexities? Saturation. Throughout the 1990s, an estimated 60 to 70 percent of all names submitted to preliminary U.S. trademark searches came back with a finding of some danger of trademark infringement. At Landor Associates and in our own consulting practices, we routinely found that the rate of rejection was 80 to 90 percent in the high-technology and telecommunication categories.[7] Some people contend that all the "good" names have been taken. We contend that all the *obvious* names were thought of again and again . . . and again. Scarcity provokes feelings of desperation. Suddenly the most bizarre Frankenstein words were being assembled, with the most exotic of spellings—words like Xosys and NetriXX. Apart from wondering about the meaning when the name is first seen, the question then becomes how do you pronounce it? Or if said aloud, how do you spell it?

These are just a few reasons the creative process alone doesn't work. Rather than establish finite rules to live or die by, we offer two Golden Guidelines of Naming:

1. If you thought of the perfect name in the first 5 minutes of trying, so did 500 other people in the last couple of decades (or days, at the height of the dot-com craze).
2. Desperation (of any sort) usually produces *merde*.

Start Your Naming Brief

So here it is—the top-secret process used by many a naming consultant broken down for you to understand and possibly attempt. The process begins not with creative ideation but rather with strategy. The reason is simple: you need a blueprint that clearly shows the tactical foundation and aesthetic and functional uniqueness of what will be presented and offered to the public.

Many of the items needed for your creative naming strategy are taken from your overall identity strategy, which was covered in Chapter 2. These are then translated into a one- to two-page document known as the "naming creative brief." A naming creative brief is divided into two halves: the first re-articulates the segments of the identity's overall positioning strategy; the second focuses on topics specific to naming. Whether you're naming a B2B technology, a new financial publishing company, or a kid's consumer product, this structure is relevant to all identities. Excerpts of a naming brief of a former B2B client are given as examples of each key section.

The brief should begin with a concisely written project summary that encapsulates what is being offered and to, whom; what the brand is currently called (if anything); any prior names; a brief description as to why name changes have occurred and are currently occurring; and any other special considerations or concerns to be noted up-front. The project summary should be brief, and clear enough that anyone from product development engineers to lay people and consultants understand what is being offered and to whom. It is the proposition pitch and perhaps price points and target markets. (Price points and target markets may also be listed separately, as appropriate to the given case.) Because the brief may circulate to everyone from project team members to ad agency managers, in-depth tech specs and short- and long-term strategic objectives should be avoided altogether. Again this is *top-level* information. The following is an actual project summary example:

Project Summary

OldProduct is infrastructure software for the wireless telecommunications industry, allowing wireless carriers to manage and deliver web-based information in multiple languages across all data-enabled devices—including PCs, Mobile Phones, Wireless PDAs, and TV Set-top Boxes—according to the preferences of the end user. Markets are worldwide.

OldProduct is currently marketed as the primary product of OldCo and will be supported in the near future by several ancillary products and services including but not limited to:

Content Catalogue	XML
SmartBar	Implementation and Support
API	Customized Content Packages

As the OldCo name is no longer appropriate for the scope and nature of the company or its products and services, our agency has been asked to create a new brand name that will identify the PME platform as well as the company (as illustrated with placeholder names below).

Company: Alpha Inc.
Platform: Alpha Preference Engine
Products: Alpha XML
             Alpha Content Catalogue
             Alpha Support

List of Competitive Names

A list of competitive names is the next section of the creative brief. This is different from an in-depth competitive analysis. Competitive names should include direct *and* indirect competitors, including any brand names that "live" in the same marketplace as your brand. The idea of the competitive names is to provide a comprehensive list of names and naming conventions to avoid in the creative process. Providing a list of descriptors and tag lines that each company is currently using is also extremely helpful as they often provide a mini-spotlight on the company's positioning and key words that that company is trying to own. While trademark searches obviously eliminate direct copycats, a little homework has to be done on the marketplace to avoid coming up with a name that actually clears registration searches but still mimics another brand name. Which brings us to the third Golden Guideline of Naming: Avoid choosing a "me-too" solution at all costs.

One sector of the dot-com demise we love to show-case is (was) the online pet sector. Petopia, e-Pets, Petsmart.com—just how many names can mimic one another and still survive as a brand? In this case, apparently only one—the one that's retail-based. Yes, the others were lousy business models with poor to no realistic profitability strategies, but we still contend that creating names that were merely variations on a theme contributed to everyone's demise. Think of it as Dr. John Nash's equilibrium theory applied to a brand: if every brand goes after the same thing, no one succeeds. Each brand, in effect, blocks another.

The following is a condensed sample from our B2B client. The actual list includes all known competitors, both direct and indirect.

Competitive Name

Oracle 9i: Application server.

Wireless Edition (formerly Oracle Portal-To-Go): A wireless infrastructure for integrating the delivery of Internet applications and data to the wireless world.

Logica: The Global Solutions company.

Openwave Systems (merger of Phone.com and Software.com): Infrastructure solutions for communications service providers.

Target Audiences

Continuing with positioning strategy, target audiences should be clearly and concisely stated in ranking order. As shown in Chapter 2, audiences can be categorized into influencers and purchasers. From a creative standpoint, a consumer-based offer vs. a business-to-business offer vs. a combination of both will alter significantly the choice of language and tone in the naming process. Here is an example from our B2B client.

Target Audiences
- Carriers
- Infrastructure (PDA, handsets, gateway, SMSC)
- Systems integrators and content developers
- Internet service providers (satellite, wireless, etc.)
- Software development
- Financial analysts/Wall Street

Features and Benefits

The next section recapitulates the brand's prioritized features and benefits to give the naming creatives a stronger sense of what the company, product, or service will offer and using what language. This language and key differentiated points can provide potential creative directions for the naming process. This example is from our B2B client.

Features

- *Information management and distribution enhancer:* Stores and manages user's preferences for information across devices
- *Server-based solution:* Easy-to-use interfaces for registering new content
- *Layered solution (modular):* Separate layer of a carrier solution that is independent of gateway, device, or presentation software
- *Open platform (APIs):* Handles virtually any type of content
- *Content catalogue:* Enables carrier to easily create suites of content targeted to specific groups of users
- *Service and support:* Ongoing, post-installation maintenance, support, and consultation

Benefits

- *Delivery personalization and simplification:* Enables carriers to build a highly targeted service for each group of users; personalized and simplified user preference management increases user loyalty and decreases user churn

- *Future insures and protects:* Separate layer increases flexibility for carriers and future insures their solution from phone technology and markup language changes
- *Ownership and control:* Enables carriers to easily expand their content offering to future requirements
- *Best of breed:* Offers flexibility to adopt best of breed solutions
- *Scalable:* Lets carriers sign new customers as quickly as the market demands
- *Speed to market:* Enables carriers to get new content up and running quickly and efficiently

Communication Attributes

Aside from the positioning statement, the communication attributes are the most important component of one's naming strategy. Why do a list of adjectives make such an impact? They are the jumping-off point for the creative ideation process. While professional naming creatives have their different styles of coming up with names, they all use the communication attributes as a starting place to create names. The adjectives become synonyms, metaphors, and mnemonic devices for evoking imagery around which to create a name. As we stressed earlier, this is all the more reason to create the most relevant, yet differentiated prioritized list of attributes. We believe in this point enough to state it once more: Avoid the usual list—"premier," "unique," "innovative," "leading," "cutting edge," and "first to market." Without a much more focused list of attributes, the naming creative process becomes equally generic, limited, and unfocused. In our example, we have two sets of communication attributes: one for the company brand and one for the platform brand. Compare the two lists. How do they describe each brand uniquely yet link synergistically to one another? The attributes will also play a crucial role in measuring results of the naming creative process.

Below are examples from our B2B client:

Company Communication Attributes

- Leading infrastructure
- Essential
- Stable
- Future driven
- Synergy
- Relevant
- Global
- Credible
- Wireless enhancer

Platform Communication Attributes

- Personalized
- Integral
- Universal
- Adaptive
- Scalable
- Enhancing

- Supporting
- Best of breed
- Simple link

Core Essence

Taking the words that describe the brand both descriptively and evocatively and culling that down to its one-, two-, or three-word core essence is the next part of the positioning and naming strategy. In some cases the core essence can be the top one or two communication attributes, and in others it is the top couple of words that describe what the offer is all about. In this case, the core essence can translate into a generic descriptor—the everyday, common way to describe a company, product, or service. The generic descriptor is essential to especially evocative and figurative names. It puts them into context. If I say "Orange," what does that mean? But if I say "Orange Telecom," the word "Orange" immediately has context. The general rule of thumb is this: The more descriptive the name, the less often a generic descriptor is needed. Once the brand has been properly established, a descriptor can eventually be dropped. For example, these are the recommended generic descriptors for our B2B client example:

Company descriptor: Wireless publishing
infrastructure

Product descriptor: Wireless publishing
                       infrastructure manager
Platform descriptor: Wireless publishing
                       infrastructure platform

Positioning Statement

The positioning statement is the next to follow. Like the overall identity strategy, the positioning statement serves as the brand's anchor and ultimately will provide a litmus test against which to measure names. Here is the positioning statement created for our B2B client. Alpha is the placeholder name.

Positioning Statement

Alpha provides information publishing infrastructure that is essential for the wireless information industry worldwide. Through its unique XML-based open technology, Alpha specializes in adaptive, integral solutions that personalize and simplify presentation and content distribution to data-enabled devices regardless of platform or language.

Naming Objectives

So far your naming creative brief includes all or most of the components of your positioning strategy: a project summary, list of competitive names, target audiences, prioritized features and benefits, communication attributes, core essence, and positioning statement. The second half of the brief contains those goals, objectives, and statements unique to naming and are aptly called the naming objectives. Naming objectives are goals to strive for and are required throughout the naming creative and selection process. These can be as broad or as narrowly focused as desired. Our B2B client's naming objectives provide examples of both general and specific objectives.

Naming Objectives

- Create unique, ownable platform name that is also a good company and product name
- Reflect positioning statement and platform communication attributes
- Balance communication of young company with mature and credible
- Appropriate for all target audiences from wireless to enterprise
- Appropriate for premium-priced products and services

Technical Parameters

Technical parameters provide a list of tactical considerations during the creative and selection process.

Geographical references, language and cultural considerations, existing brand guidelines and nomenclature goals are just a few technical parameters. We like to include in this section words or topics to clearly avoid during the naming process because of competition, overuse, stigmas in the industry, or personal preferences in the company. The following technical parameters are for our B2B client:

Technical Parameters

- Company name will be registered in multiple international markets, including Asia, Western Europe, Southeast Asia, Brazil, Argentina, Chile, Mexico, Canada, Australia.
- Name will be accompanied by generic descriptor (e.g., Personalized Wireless Infrastructure).
- AVOID Net, Internet, Web, world, and otherwise "Internet-sounding" names such as words ending in .com or beginning with i- or e-.
- AVOID names with an irreverent tone.

Preliminary Creative Directions

The final section of the naming creative brief is the preliminary creative directions. This list can be as sparse or as comprehensive as desired. The main objective to bear in mind is that these are listed to get the creative process started. These directions may be from personal inspiration or sparked by a comment made by the CEO. They should never be presented as the only directions to explore. The last thing creativity requires is a box around it. The list below from our B2B client gives just a few examples.

Preliminary Creative Directions

- Explore coined English and foreign language names.
- Explore musical metaphors, imagery, words.
- Explore geological (layer, granite, etc.) metaphors, imagery, words.

Once completed, the creative brief should be reviewed with a very fine tooth comb. We cannot iterate enough how important it is for the brief to be accurate factually and with the language and tone clearly defined and accepted by those approving the naming process. There has been more than one case in naming history of a lot of time and energy put into creating names only to have them presented to a decision maker who never approved either selected portions of the document or the whole thing. Naming is a long, tedious process. Gaining the designated decision maker's input and buy-in at this stage can save thousands or even millions of dollars in lost time and expenses.

Creating Words

Alycia is often asked what makes her naming process unique and valuable. Her answer is invariably strategy plus creativity. The creative brief is the key to producing relevant, differentiated, and intriguing solutions. In her practice, she subcontracts marketing and advertising writers who have a proven track record in the naming realm. These are the people who actually come up with the lists of names to be considered. Why does she usually hire copywriters? They have the linguistic talent and marketing awareness that provide the most appropriate selections to choose from. In general writers who lack a marketing background or who don't at least have marketing savvy don't provide as many viable options. The naming team is usually a balance of seasoned pros with one or two junior writers—those writers just starting out in marketing. Every writer has a particular forte. Some are particularly gifted with creative high-tech names, others with children's product names. No one writer is superb at everything. Knowing a writer's style and credentials is critical. One of the added values we provide as consultants is to know our teams' strengths and weaknesses and delegate accordingly. If you're taking on the naming process in-house, evaluate your freelance namers as carefully as you would your internal team members. Use freelance namers as often as possible either exclusively or in combination with in-house people. A freelancer offers experience and objectivity. Using only in-house people dilutes the much-needed objectivity in this process. A combination of freelance and in-house people generally yields richer results.

The Long and Short Lists

The results of each namer's work should be transferred to a master list of names. Think of it as the one-stop archive for everything thought of. The master list of names can and should be several pages long, with literally hundreds of names on it. If yours comes out to five pages with double-spaced words in 20-point type, you know you have a lot more work to do. Is it simply a matter of more is better? Yes and no. The master list when first reviewed will generally produce a groan. A lot of the obvious, clichéd, and totally inappropriate names will be on that list—it's a given in nearly any creative process. What will also be on the list (or so we hope) are a number of viable choices. When it comes to trademark availability searches, the more viable choices the better. So how does one decide on that initial list? Your entire naming team should gather to review what has been created, the rationale behind certain selections (such as etymology or significance), and what should be put into the keeper pile—the short list. Compare the names to the communication attributes. Which ones suggest one to two of the top attributes? We suggest eliminating those that don't suggest any attributes listed. Insert the name into the positioning statement. Does the name "fit"? During this process, certain names will be intriguing, neutral, or completely despised. The beauty of a team-based critique process is that by discussing the names and rationales, new ideas will be sparked and new names created as a result.

The Trademark Process

Once the short list of names is compiled, it's ready to be sent out for preliminary U.S. trademark availability searches. Most naming firms and consultants do not have an in-house trademark lawyer to run these searches. However, experienced consultants can offer an outside trademark attorney or law firm and walk the client through the process, acting as a liaison between the two. Retaining an experienced trademark attorney makes an enormous difference to the trademark process. Yes, they cost more than, say, running searches through various subscription-based databases, but the results will be interpreted much more precisely and definitively. In the long run, we feel the fees are worth it. We can't make this point enough. We've worked with all possible sources through the trademark process only to have some clients learn the hard way: they should have forked out the extra money for a trademark attorney.

The preliminary searches are just that: the first cursory pass at comparing each individual name submitted against what is already registered within the same categories. We could go on about all the different trademark classifications and the pros, cons, and trends in trademark law, but frankly that's another book.

Once the results are back, you will generally hear a yes, no, and maybe. These translate as: yes, there is a possibility this name could perhaps be trademarked; maybe, there's a possibility, but it could encounter some problems; and no way unless of course you're willing to negotiate with the owners of a name to buy it outright. Whatever the outcome, you will want as many names in the yes and maybe camp as possible since, as we said, these are just preliminary U.S.

searches. International trademark searches and final searches are yet more obstacles to overcome, and both are especially costly ones. If there aren't enough potentially available choices, it's back to the creative drawing board.

Cultural and Linguistic Analysis

Before stepping into international trademark searches, we recommend conducting cultural and linguistic analysis on the potential name candidates. As we discussed in Chapter 2, this is a crucial step when you are stepping out beyond American borders. In this day and age, it is important for domestic brands as well, because of the number of Spanish and Asian language speakers in the United States.

The first thing to realize is that cultural is different from linguistic. Cultural checks out a name for cultural meanings, perceptions, and nuances. A German-speaking person who has lived in the United States most of his life will likely not get the pop cultural significance of a word to the same degree as a native German speaker. Trends come and go and it takes a native to be aware of them. Linguistic analysis checks the name for classical or traditional meanings. Both processes ensure that a name isn't offensive, unintentionally humorous, or otherwise inappropriate both as the literal name and as a possible translation; remember our Nova example. On the plus side, a name may be found to have positive messages that reinforce the brand even further in that market or language. (This doesn't happen very often.) What is desired is a name that comes out neutral. Communication can then be built into the brand through descriptors, tag lines, and messaging that is in the native tongue and appropriate for that specific market.

Don't forget to include checks of widely spoken languages based on individual countries. For example, American English has quite a lot of slang words that differ altogether from British, Australian, or Canadian English. The same goes for Spanish spoken in Mexico, Argentina, and Spain or French spoken in Canada, France, or Mozambique. This may seem like an awful lot of time and trouble to go through, but considering the alternatives, it's worth the research.

The reason for conducting cultural and linguistic analysis before undertaking any necessary international searches is an economic one. It's far more cost-efficient to check several names at once for appropriateness than checking for international trademark searches.

The International Trademark Game

International trademark searches come in three garden varieties: WISS (worldwide identical screening search), RISS (regional identical screening search), and country by country. The last is the most appropriate if you only plan to investigate a couple of extra markets for trademark availability. All are offered through Thomson and Thomson trademark and copyright services. The RISS searches larger regions, such as the European Union. The WISS is the most comprehensive, but unfortunately it is reputed to be the least accurate. Because the trademark laws vary from country to country, it's simply impossible to have a 100 percent accurate account of all trademarks held everywhere. When venturing into international trademark waters, go cautiously and with the assistance of a highly experienced trademark attorney. Also know that it is not uncommon to have different brand names for different countries based on trademark registration challenges.

A classic example of international trademark intrigue is the ongoing battle between Anheuser-Busch and a small Czech brewer based in Ceske Budejovice called Budweiser Budvar, a company dating back to

1895. Budweiser is historically the name of a beer appellation brewed in the Czech town of Budweis, which dates back to 1265. For centuries the word Budweiser has been used as a guarantee of origin for beers brewed in Bohemia. By the fifteenth century, the town was home to 44 breweries. When two German immigrants named Eberhard Anheuser and Augustus Busch decided to brew an American pale beer in the style of Czech Pilsner and Budweiser in 1876, they claimed the name Budweiser and in 1890 proclaimed the product the "King of Beers." The latter was a spin on King Ferdinand I's 1547 proclamation that a Budweis beer brewed especially for him be called "Beer of Kings." Despite the historical significance and heritage, Anheuser-Busch was determined to own Budweiser as a brand name and blocked the Czech company in 1939 from using Bud, Budweis, or Budweiser in any location north of the Panama Canal. The two companies have been engaged in legal battles for more than a century over the use of the famous Budweiser name all over the world. When Budweiser Budvar decided to export their beer to North America, the name of the product was changed to Czechvar, a portmanteau of Czech and *pivovar*, the Czech word for beer, to comply with U.S. trademark laws. However in several countries, it's still known as Budweiser Budvar. England is the only country where both products can be sold under the name Budweiser. According to an article written in 2001 by David Protz, Budweiser Budvar has 380 trademark registrations in over 101 countries. At the time, they were involved in 40 court cases and 40 patent administrative proceedings, all with Anheuser-Busch.[8]

Selecting a Name

A significant number of name candidates are weeded out by the trademark and cultural-linguistic searches. Before entering the final trademark search process, you'll want at least two names and one or two alternates. Remember, one name can always fall out of the race, and it's best to have other options. Fear and deadlock can creep in at two points in the naming process: right before trademark searches and right after. These points lead to the inevitable selection process, and each time there are fewer choices and fewer chances to mess up. Emotions tend to run high because the stakes are high. Suddenly a name choice that seemed perfect on Tuesday seems as palatable as mincemeat today. The point is, erratic emotions and vacillating choices are a natural part of the process. Key to keeping the process on track is to always go back to the original naming strategy. Look at the communication attributes again. How many key attributes does that name convey or suggest? Look at the positioning statement. Insert the name candidate into the positioning statement. Does it fulfill the positioning requirements as stated? Is it convincing? Is it easy and pleasant to say? Alycia's favorite litmus test is perhaps the most low-tech of all: pretend you're the receptionist and have to answer the phone with the new name. "Good morning, ThisIsAFantasticName Technologies. May I help you?" If you want to go even further, insert a few name choices into recent or dummy press releases (provided they reflect the new identity positioning).

There are several other techniques we can suggest, but at the end of the day, no name is perfect, no name will convey all the communication attributes listed, and in the final analysis, what separates a winner from a loser is conviction.

THE YIN AND YANG
OF VISUAL IDENTITIES

When the brand's positioning and verbal identity have been completed, the next step is to create the visual identity. In essence, this means creating a visual representation of the positioning and verbal identity.

The visual identity has four purposes: The first is to bring the brand to life by giving character and personality to the positioning and name. The second is to enhance brand recognition and recall. The third assists in to differentiate the brand from the competition. The fourth is to tie all the disparate brand elements together with the same look and feel.

Visual identities are far more than just a logo. A visual identity consists of an integrated system of visual cues that include colors, shapes, and typography. These fundamental elements are combined in unique and creative ways to establish a proprietary brand signature (a.k.a. logo), packaging structures and graphics, retail environments, advertising, marketing and promotional materials, vehicles, signage, uniforms, and so on. These elements together make up the total visual identity.

From a philosophical point of view, we believe in simplicity, simplicity, simplicity. Like naming, the more complex the design system is, the longer it takes your target audience to recognize, understand, and recall the identity.

While there are numerous books on the market that go into the philosophy, creation, and technicalities of design, the purpose of this chapter is to introduce the basic elements and process of designing a visual identity. Here we define the individual components of an identity system and the steps we recommend to create an identity. While design can be rather technical, especially when applying the identity to specific formats, it is generally the part of the identity process that people enjoy most.

Visual Basics

Figure 4–1 shows the basic elements of visual vocabulary, which include the signature, the logotype, the logomark, the wordmark, generic descriptors, and tag lines.

The Signature

The signature is the combination of the logomark, the logotype, and the tag line. Not all companies use all three elements: Some may use a combination of logotype and logomark. Others may just use typography, modified to be proprietary and distinctive (e.g., Yahoo, Coca-Cola, Kellogg's). This unique treatment of typography is called a wordmark.

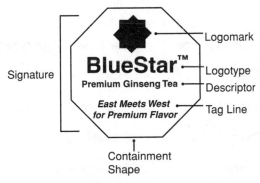

Figure 4–1. Visual identity components.

The Logotype

The logotype should be in a typeface (also called a font) that assists in defining the character and personality of the brand. Typography is an art in and of itself—there are scores of books on the subject and thousands of typefaces to choose from. Before beginning the design process, it's essential to know where your brand will live. If it is to be printed on a microchip, it needs to be extremely simple in order to be visible and readable. The same is true for logotypes at the opposite end of the size spectrum—for billboards or stadium signage. The common theme here is readability. The faster consumers can read and understand a brand, the faster they will recognize and remember it.

Typefaces come in two styles, serif and sans serif. (See Figure 4–2.) Serif typefaces have extra strokes—

Serif Typefaces	Sans Serif Typefaces
Example 1	Example 1
Example 2	Example 2
Example 3	Example 3
Example 4	Example 4

Figure 4–2. Serif and sans serif typefaces.

little feet or stems on the letters—whereas sans serif type is without the embellishments.

Even with the small sample of typefaces shown in Figure 4–2, it's easy to see the variation in character and personality. Serif typefaces are generally used for the body text of periodicals and books (like the one in this book) because they are easier to read in paragraph form. When used as a logotype, serif typefaces are considered more conservative, sophisticated, elegant, and authoritative in appearance. They are regularly used to represent financial businesses, law firms, and other traditional institutions.

Sans serif typefaces are generally used for headlines in newspapers, in web site heads, and on signage because they stand out better. Most logotypes use sans serif typefaces because they are considered cleaner, simpler, more contemporary and friendly. You can modify the character of an identity by changing the case of the type font. The options range from capitals (caps) to lowercase (see Figure 4–3.)

In general, capital letters convey strength, power, and authority, while lower case letters convey simplicity and approachability. Figure 4–4 shows our fictional BlueStar brand in various typefaces.

Once a primary typeface has been selected for the logotype, it can be used in marketing materials for headlines or even body copy in brochures. We recom-

Serif	Sans Serif
ALL CAPS	ALL CAPS
SMALL CAPS	SMALL CAPS
Initial Caps	Initial Caps
lower case	lower case
BLUESTAR	BLUESTAR
BLUESTAR	BLUESTAR
BlueStar	BlueStar
bluestar	bluestar

Figure 4–3. Comparison of serif and sans serif typefaces.

mend selecting a secondary complementary typeface used across signage and marketing materials. The concept of using a complementary font provides a visual juxtaposition between typefaces. A brand name or wordmark using a serif typeface is often complemented by a sans serif typeface in the descriptor or tag line. A sans serif typeface usually requires a serif typeface for correspondence and marketing materials such as brochures and web sites. These typefaces must be applied consistently across all branded materials to create a strong look and feel. Apple Computer has done an excellent job of using the Garamond

Serif	Sans Serif
BLUESTAR	***BLUESTAR***
BLUESTAR	BLUESTAR
BlueStar	BlueStar
bluestar	**bluestar**

Figure 4–4. Examples of Bluestar identity in different typefaces and cases.

typeface as a primary logotype and a corporate type-face for all its marketing and promotional materials.

The Logomark

A logomark is a symbol that is used in combination with the logotype to create a distinctive and memorable visual identity. Logomarks can range from realistic to abstract, from organic to graphic. Examples are shown in Figure 4–5.

At Landor Associates, we were often approached with the request to "just make us a logo like Nike." Our response was, "No problem—all we need is a billion dollars and twenty years." Our tongue-in-cheek reply illustrates the fact that a logo alone will not make a brand. Because Nike has been doggedly consistent in applying this simple identity in advertising, promotions, sports events, on the field of play, and on key players, the company has reached a rare status: it

Figure 4–5. Sample logomarks. Reprinted with permission of McDonald's and Viacom.

can drop the company name and just use its logomark. (In case you were wondering, the original Nike logomark was created by a student at Portland State University for $35.)

The Wordmark

The wordmark is typography that has been modified to be more proprietary and distinctive. Wordmarks are generally created as an alternative to the logomark-logotype combination because they are clean and simple. Essentially, the wordmark *becomes* the logomark. Some of the modifications can be simple color changes and graphic modifications, as with the Mobil Oil, Microsoft, or Xerox identities, or more complex graphic treatments, as with the Hyatt or

Kmart identities. Coca-Cola uses its original Spencerian script with its famous "wave" (formally known as the Dynamic Ribbon Device, or DRD for short). Figure 4–6 shows some examples of wordmarks.

Generic Descriptor

As we explained in Chapter 3, the generic descriptor is the everyday, common way to describe a company, product, or service. Food and beverage products require a simple, descriptive word or words with clear meanings to define the product category. For example:

- Cereal
- Spring water
- Cough syrup
- Carbonated beverage
- Sunblock lotion

Some brands use evocative words to differentiate the product in a proprietary way. For example:

Figure 4–6. Sample wordmarks. Reprinted with permission of FedEx, Yahoo!, and Viacom.

- Mountain-grown coffee
- Hand-picked grapes
- Slow-roasted beans
- Thirst quencher

Tag Lines and Strap Lines

Tag lines help to define brand name, company focus, or positioning. Particularly for new brands we recommend that the tag line be "locked up" both verbally and visually with the brand name as often as possible to help clarify and position the brand. The tag line is usually subordinate in size and location to the brand name, so it doesn't interfere visually with the name. Subsidiaries and divisions with names different from the corporate parent name may require the use of a legal strap line identifying ownership. Strap lines use the same subordinate structural treatment as tag lines. These identifiers may also be used for parent-company endorsements to leverage equity from the parent company. Some examples are shown in Figure 4–7.

The World of Color

People remember visual elements in the following order: color, shapes, letters, numbers. The first two

Figure 4–7. Examples of strap lines.

are visceral energies, and the second two are analytical data. Our physical beings respond immediately to colors and shapes, and then our mind processes the data. This has been shown time and again with some of the world's largest brands: Coca-Cola red, McDonald's Golden Arches, IBM's Big Blue, Kodak yellow, Tiffany pale blue, and so on. Owning a color as a mnemonic device for your brand significantly reinforces recognition and recall.

In 1991–1992, David Wisnom worked on a variety of projects for Coca-Cola in Europe, including the 1992 Madrid Olympics and World Expo '92 in Seville. One of the projects in Spain was developing a decision matrix to determine the most strategic locations for "Points of Red" which meant, yes, points of Coca-Cola red. The concept was to identify high traffic areas where Coca-Cola could place vending machines, billboards, tables and umbrellas, signage as a point of sale or brand impression all based upon the brand color. Coca-Cola is identified as one of the most recognized brands in the world, and this is not by accident. It is extremely consistent in its application of its brand and the use of its proprietary Coke red. The company has developed a strict set of standards for the application of its red on virtually any substrate, so it appears the same each time. Its application and use is so effective that Alycia's son could recognize Coke consistently by the tender age of 2. The Coca-Cola signature and proprietary red is also one of the best protected. Insiders at Coca-Cola joke that their trademark law department is a corporate profit center.

Like Coca-Cola, McDonald's presence is ubiquitous. The consistent use of its red-and-yellow signage throughout the world has created a recognizable flag for would-be consumers craving french fries in the Hinterlands. Even if the sign reads in the native language, you know that it is still McDonald's, a brand that you can count on.

Pepperidge Farm is another great example in the consumer product category that has taken special care to own a color. Ironically in this case, the color is white. Pepperidge Farm uses white on all its cookie and cracker packaging, creating a billboard effect of a block of white in a retail environment. With the image overload of multiple brands and multiple offerings on store shelves, it stands out, making the selection process easier for the consumer. If you have two crying kids in a shopping cart, anything that will shorten your time and theirs in the store is usually beneficial. If you know to look for white first when shopping for cookies, then for your specific flavor, this reduces the selection process to a mere two steps. Simplifying the selection process has the potential to create stronger brand loyalty.

In the petroleum category, color and design in the retail environment make a difference to consumers who may be traveling at high speeds and at night. Think of the various stations around the country— Shell, Chevron, Amoco, Mobil, BP, Union 76, Texaco. They all have specific color systems ranging from red, white, and blue to green, to orange, to yellow, red, and gray. Shell Oil, for example, designed its stations to appeal to women: they are extremely well lit at night and their large, open filling areas appear friendly, safe, and inviting. The yellow-red-gray color scheme stands out in daylight, and especially at night. The colors act as a mnemonic prompt of the brand's positive qualities or attributes.

Color Psychology

Color is light and light is energy. Scientists have found that actual physiological changes take place in human beings when they are exposed to certain colors. Colors can stimulate, excite, depress, tranquilize, increase appetite, and create a feeling of warmth or coolness.

Our personal and cultural associations affect our experience of color. Colors are seen as warm or cool mainly because of long-held associations. Associations come from both natural and cultural references. Yellow, orange, and red are associated with the heat of the sun and fire, while blue, green, and violet are associated with the coolness of leaves, the sea, and the sky. Warm colors seem closer to the viewer than cool colors, but when used in certain combinations vivid cool colors can overwhelm subtle, warm colors. Using warm colors for foreground and cool colors for background enhances the perception of depth and therefore dimension.

Red, yellow, and orange are generally considered high-arousal colors, while blue, green, and most violets are low-arousal hues. However, the brilliance, darkness, and lightness of a color can alter the psychological message significantly. While a light blue-green appears to be tranquil, wet, and cool, a brilliant turquoise, often associated with a lush tropical ocean setting, is more exciting to the eye. Colors act upon the body as well as the mind. Red has been shown to stimulate the senses and raise the blood pressure, while blue has the opposite effect and calms the mind. The psychological association of a color is often more meaningful than the visual experience. Black and white can be quite elegant in combination. Although black can seem funereal or mysterious, it's the clothing "color of choice" for hip people and designers. It's associated with elegance, black-tie affairs (e.g., the San Francisco Black & White Ball), black limousines, and so on. In our culture white is often thought of as sterile. Like black and gray, white is neutral and supports any color. It is associated with weddings, virginity, innocence, and purity. It is also used as a cue for products in the pharmaceutical, health, and beauty categories as well as for diet foods.

Shapes and Structures

The Absolut bottle, the Transamerica Building, OXO Good Grips, the Golden Arches, and the Goodyear blimp are just a few examples of shapes and structures that, like color, act as mnemonic devices to support, define, or differentiate a brand. Although the Goodyear blimp has nothing to do with tires directly, its image is synonymous with the brand. This is an example of indirect association. The Golden Arches, which have become an integral component of the McDonald's brand identity, are an example of direct association: Even the word "arches" is synonymous with the restaurant chain. Let's look at how shapes and structures can affect a brand identity either directly or indirectly.

Beverages

Traditionally, distilled spirits, aperitifs, and wines appeared in different structures to differentiate and create desired perceptions. The distilled spirits category uses unique structures on bottles to differentiate brands so that they stand out on the crowded shelves of a bar or pub. The shape of the Absolut has been used to create one of the most popular and consistent ad campaigns in recent years.

One of the most famous bottle shapes is, of course, the Coca-Cola contour bottle. The contour bottle is so much a part of the brand presentation that the flintglass bottle is recognized worldwide even without graphics. It fell out of production in the United States because of the demand for plastic bottles and the desire to cut costs on shipping, but it can still be found in any European café. In fact, the contour bottle has been reintroduced in the United States, this time in plastic, as a nostalgic retro package. It's been a huge hit—so much so that Coca-Cola designed an illustration of the contour bottle to place on its aluminum cans as part of the overall product design. In the early 1990s, Coca-Cola even experimented at making contour cans. Needless to say, this particular execution never quite topped the original success.

Architecture

Chicago, New York, and San Francisco are just a few of the major cities that can be easily recognized by their skylines. Think of the Sears Tower in Chicago, the TransAmerica Building in San Francisco, the Empire State Building in New York, even the St. Louis Arch and the Seattle Space Needle. Think of tourist destinations such as Epcot Center and Disneyland. All of these structures have become icons for their city or destination and, like the proprietary logomark, serve as mnemonic devices. Some building shapes and design elements have actually become corporate logomarks: for example, the TransAmerica Corporation or the Magic Kingdom at Disneyland. The McDonald's Golden Arches are an example of direct association. They originated with the building and signage used for the first restaurant, which opened in 1955 in Des Plaines, Illinois. Today they are an integral component of the corporate identity system, the signage on over 29,000 restaurants, designs on toys, packaging graphics, and even the handles on the Happy Meals box introduced in 1979.

Consumer Products

One of the great consumer product success stories of the last decade is OXO International Good Grips from Copco, now a subsidiary of World Kitchen. The distinctive line of black-handled kitchen utensils were originally developed for people with arthritis. The handles followed universal design concepts to create ergonomically designed, transgenerational tools that appeal to the broadest possible market. The design includes nonslip, black rubber oval handles with thumb and forefinger grips. What was planned as a small line of specialty products has turned into a line of over 300 products, all sporting the same appealing contemporary ergonomic design. The unique design invites the consumer to pick one up just to see how it feels. These quality products are two to three times as expensive as similar products, but many home chefs consider them worth it. This is an example of innovative product design creating a greater perceived value.

Technology

The Apple iMac, which was introduced in the late 1990s, actually leveraged the heritage of the original 1984 Macintosh. The Macintosh's self-contained unit—CPU, monitor, and disk drive all in one—supported the product positioning of "easy to use." The compelling product design of the iMacs reinforced and personalized this ease-of-use concept. From the start, the Macintosh's graphic user interface had emphasized user-friendliness. Now with the iMac, the introduction of a choice of five bold colors applied to a single contained shape shook up the PC marketplace instantly. Finally—a sleek computer that wasn't a neutral beige, gray, or black! Soon a bevy of peripherals and a handful of computer manufacturers jumped into the color chassis act to capitalize on its popularity. The 2002 iMac is as simple as it gets—a totally contained igloo-shaped CPU and CD/DVD drive, with a flexible arm supporting a flat screen. The iMac is a true marriage of form and function as desktop art.

The Design Process

Clients often want to start the design process either before the naming development is completed or while it is still going on. We always advise our clients to wait because the brand name drives so much of the visual creative process that it is much more productive to select the name first. Specific imagery, tone, and style can be derived from different names. Consider the following names: Laser and Sunfish. They are both small one- to two-person sailboats about the same size, yet each evokes entirely different imagery and tone. Laser is more technical and precision-oriented, whereas Sunfish conveys a more colorful, playful image. The Laser is positioned to attract serious sailors and racers as a performance sailboat. The Sunfish is positioned to attract families and kids for summer fun and easy-to-operate sailboating. Although a designer can have a lot of positioning strategy information and/or a naming creative brief, this information alone is simply not enough. The actual name, supported by the positioning strategy, drives design development.

Completing the Design Brief

A design brief is a document that guides both the creative team of designers and the decision makers. It restates each component of the positioning strategy and, like the naming brief, provides additional information specific to the design process, for example, design objectives, technical parameters, and creative directions to pursue. Using the format we outlined in Chapter 3, here are sections from a client's actual design brief document. The first sections follow the same format as in the naming brief, including the project summary and all applicable positioning strategy information. The brief was done early in the company's history. As with many technology companies, its product strategy and positioning has changed to reflect its evolving markets. However, its corporate identity endures.

Project Summary

Alchemedia is a technology company whose key product provides image management and content commercialization for owners of digital content on the Internet. Alchemedia's product is an Internet browser control that gives a company the ability to offer richer, better content as well as larger-scale images by enabling control/management of proprietary, high-value content—particularly static images— over the Net. While currently the click of the mouse can save most GIF images from a web site to one's desktop, Alchemedia's product enables the web site owner to display images on the Net without giving them away, either by disallowing access altogether or by managing it, such as requiring user information before allowing access.

Alchemedia's future version is a commerce application that in effect allows proprietary images to be turned into merchandising options. For example, a Net user can choose a selected Tweetie Bird image from Warner Bros.' web site to be transferred onto a mug, T-shirt, or poster for X dollars. The multiversion product line will be offered as an Internet service and as a server version.

Target Audiences

The purchasers of products will be content developers and providers

For Internet Product

>   Professional photographers
>   Small businesses
>   Individuals with personal homepages

For Server Product

>   Film Studios (e.g., Disney, Warner Bros.)
>   Publications (e.g., *Playboy, National Geographic*)
>   Photo stock houses

Medium to large companies with proprietary
digital content such as web-based catalogues
ISPs or community sites (e.g., Geocities, UUNet)

Target Audiences: Profile

Director of production or networks
Director of online presence, commerce
Intellectual, trademark, or property lawyer
Business development
Brand manager
Product manager
Small business owners
Small site developers
Image librarian

Communication Attributes

Enriching
Contemporary, fresh, dynamic
Credible, trustworthy
Friendly, approachable
Innovative, cutting edge
Easy to use
Flexible
End-user driven, business-oriented
Stable
American

Following the lead in this example, additional positioning information such as features and benefits, positioning statement, and core essence should be added to the design brief to guide subsequent design development and to provide a framework against which design choices will be evaluated.

Competitive Visual Practices

A visual audit of competitive companies provides the opportunity to show the visual practices of corporate and brand identities, marketing collateral, advertising, web sites, products, etc. We recommend selecting at least three to four core competitors to provide a contextual framework of the competitive marketplace. These competitive materials provide the foundation for specific category cues, colors and shapes, general strengths and weaknesses, design directions to avoid, and opportunities to pursue. The competitive materials should be grouped by company to determine if the competitor has a cohesive look and feel, and whether the competitor applies its identity consistently across all marketing, sales, and promotional materials.

Design Objectives

Similar to the naming objectives, design objectives serve as a guide for designers in the creative process and as a benchmark for selection. These can be broadly or narrowly focused, depending on the need. The goal of design objectives is to articulate how the general look and feel should be conveyed to the target audience. Most of the objectives are derived from the core essence, the features and benefits, and communication attributes: for example, mature versus youthful; exudes credibility; appears conservative versus trendy; premium-priced and sophisticated.

Design Objectives

- Develop a compelling signature and logomark for Alchemedia.
- Translate signature to other products.
- Base logomark design platform on the concept of alchemy (see enclosed information), the transmutation of one thing to another of greater value, i.e., base metal to gold, or in this case, a static picture to sellable commerce item.
- Utilize elements of the corporate logomark for the platform/product name.
- Ensure logomark works as a co-brand and as a button for the web sites.
- Create a strong wordmark for Alchemedia and more organic logomark for the product name.

Technical Parameters

Technical parameters provide a list of tactical issues to consider during the creative and selection process. Cultural considerations such as potentially offensive colors and shapes, existing brand guidelines, various applications of the identity to billboards and signage or miniature applications such as microchips, horizontal-only applications, translations, limitations of the number of colors, etc., are just a few common technical parameters to consider.

Technical Parameters

The Alchemedia identity will be applied to a variety of media, including print, signage, and electronic. This will require flexibility in the design to be applied via offset printing, silkscreen printing, embroidery, and office printers, as well as on the web site.

Color applications will include business papers such as business cards, stationery, folders, brochures, signage, and embroidered shirts and hats. The color applications may range from four-color process to one-color silkscreen and must be translatable to a web site.

Black and white versions include: business forms, fax cover sheets, etc.

Visual identity should be versatile enough to be easily readable on a billboard and on a key fob.

Be conscious of number of colors and its effect on the cost of applications.

Preliminary Creative Directions

Preliminary creative directions may include some of the metaphors used in the naming brief or specific directions that may be reflective of the brand name, product, or service. In the case of our fictitious Blue-Star product example, the figurative communication of the name is one obvious literal direction to follow. Other creative directions may include graphical treatments such as color ranges, an organic free-flowing design, or a hard edged logomark typography.

In addition to the basic design brief information, any other information that can stimulate the visual appetite of the designers is highly beneficial—related history, name etymology, related visuals, etc. Our design team was given the following additional information regarding "alchemy," which was the basis for the Alchemedia corporate name.

Additional Information

alchemy (àl´ke-mê) noun

1. A medieval chemical philosophy having as its asserted aims the transmutation of

base metals into gold, the discovery of the panacea, and the preparation of the elixir of longevity.

2. A seemingly magical power or process of transmuting: "He wondered by what alchemy it was changed, so that what sickened him one hour, maddened him with hunger the next." (Marjorie K. Rawlings)

Middle English *alkamie,* from Old French *alquemie,* from Medieval Latin *alchymia,* from Arabic *al-kìmiyâ'*: *al,* the + *kìmiyâ',* chemistry (from Late Greek *khêmeia, khumeia,* perhaps from Greek *Khêmia*).

- ■ alchem´ical (àl-kèm´-î-kel) or alchem´ic, adjective.
- ■ conversion: chemistry, alchemy.
- ■ occultism: secret art, esoteric science, occult lore, alchemy, astrology, psychomancy, spiritualism, magic, sorcery.

Alchemy was the ancient art devoted to discovering a substance to transmute common metals into gold. Although it was dubious and often illusory, alchemy was the predecessor of chemistry.

Figure 4–8. Alchemedia identity. Reprinted with permission of Alchemedia.

This additional background information on alchemy went on about the brief history of alchemy and provided relevant web sites for further research. This provided inspiration to the design team to conduct further research into symbology and metaphors about alchemy. As a result, the symbols in the final logomark portion of the signature are from a sixteenth-century painting. (See Figure 4–8.)

Creative Exploration

As we stated in previous chapters, it is imperative to receive buy-in and approval from the designated decision makers at each stage and for every aspect of the design brief. Failure to do so leads more often than not to lost time, money, and tempers. Once the design brief has been blessed by the powers that be, the design team is briefed and creative exploration begins first as a collective conceptual effort and then individually. Exploration generally includes stand-alone symbols, as well as proprietary logotypes and wordmarks. The first round of design is very general and usually directional in nature, and may include dozens to hundreds of designs depending on the scope of the project and the size of the design team. Most design firms will have interim design "crits" or critiques to narrow the direction and focus on the most promising designs. At this juncture, designers will begin refining selected design directions, which may include typography, logomarks, and color.

Although the true test of a visual identity is how it appears in black (think fax and photocopy), color is what really brings the identity to life. Picture Campbell's soup in white-and-chartreuse cans or Stanley Works tools in pink! The color selection changes your perception of each brand immediately. Color is one of the most critical ingredients of the overall identity. Remember, it is the primary mnemonic device of an identity system. The first place to start in determining your brand's color range is the brand identity strategy document. The target audience profile begins to paint the picture of what might be relevant to the audience. The positioning and brand persona begin to define the personality and character you want to convey. And the communication attributes assist in rounding out the potential directions.

How Many Colors?

The basic rule of thumb for identity systems is this: The more the colors, the more costly it is to reproduce them, the greater potential there is for mistakes, and the more difficult it is to manage consistency. But often first impressions really do count: If you only want to pay for two colors and the identity really "sings" in three, springing for the additional color can be worth it.

Avoid Trendy Colors

It is a mistake to select a color based upon current trends. Once the trend is over, so is your identity. Think of all the orange identities over the past few years that appeared, especially in the tech sector. Because of the sheer numbers, all at once there were serious differentiation issues. Look for rich, enduring colors that assist in defining your brand's positioning. Consider what will work for the company today and five years from today.

Beware of Custom Colors

Some designers will push for custom colors to be "unique, cutting-edge, and differentiated." This can lead to disaster in trying to maintain consistency across all potential applications because of the complexity of mixing colors. Printers need very talented people and specialized equipment to mix and maintain inks for each printing run, whether local or across the world. The chance of production problems occurring and inconsistent applications are magnified exponentially with custom colors. For simplicity and global consistency, we recommend using the Pantone system.

Color by Application

As we mentioned earlier, it's important to clearly understand where your identity will live. Colors vary by application and by substrate (the material that ink or paint is applied to, such as newsprint for newspapers, glossy paper for brochures, metal cans, plastic packaging, or a vinyl banner). When managing the color consistency of your new identity, be sure to understand the effects of different printing techniques, such as rotogravure, offset, flexography, and silkscreen printing. Each produces variable results because of the different inks, plates, or screens used. Also, the material or substrate that you print on is critical: the finer the paper, the better reproduction of colors. A simple test is to place several different grades of paper in a desktop color printer and print the same design on each. You should see the difference clearly. Knowing how and where your new visual identity will be applied before its creation will prevent many headaches in the long run.

In addition to the paper world, you should also consider additional applications such as signage, uniforms, vehicles, billboards. These types of applications can indicate potential flaws in the design system: difficult to read in small applications, colors blended together in dark spaces, the design system looks great on a uniform and terrible on a web page, and so on. Several years ago a signage program was created for a bank in Michigan where one of the key technical parameters was that the final colors must stand out under gray skies. Why? Because in that part of Michigan there were only about 80 days of sunshine a year, so the color selection that could have maximum impact was highly critical. The bottom line is, test the potential color applications throughout the design process.

Selecting Identities

Once the final internal critique is completed, three to four final solutions should be selected that best reflect the design brief and identity strategy. These full-color designs should be presented in isolation in various sizes to demonstrate readability. In addition, the designs should be shown in context in a sample application such as business card, letterhead, or product label. The design team should provide the rationale behind each design direction to clarify the designer's vision. An honest, tactful, and firm discussion about the work's strengths and weaknesses should be used when evaluating design work. It's business, not a personal matter. Your company is paying for it, and it could mean the success of your brand.

The purpose of a work session is to select the most compelling one to two identities to refine. Selecting the final designs can be a difficult process or a virtual no-brainer. A good deal of the decision-making process is visceral. "Design A is the one, it really jumps off the page." or "I hate design C because I don't like orange." While this is human nature, we recommend as much as possible basing design evaluations upon the components of the design brief. How do the design recommendations measure up against the criteria set by the positioning strategy, design objectives, and technical parameters? We have always found strategy to be a much more objective litmus test than decisions based on gut feelings about a color because you had a bad experience with it when you were 12 years old.

Identity Refinement

Once at least two designs are selected for refinement, the design team and client should agree to specific design refinements such as color modifications, proportional changes, typography alternatives, and logomark alterations. Occasionally, two designs are combined: for example, the type from design A and the logomark from design C. The refinements should be documented and signed off by you and the client prior to beginning the refinement process. We generally recommend pursuing two different design directions for better comparison purposes, as well as for optional during-design research. On occasion, one design may be selected, but multiple iterations should be pursued to identify the best solution. As the refinements are completed, the designs can be applied to additional prototypes such as signage and web sites to assure that they are readable and that the color remains consistent across the various applications.

At least two refined solutions should be presented to you in context via sample applications such as business cards, sample web site homepage, brochure cover, label on a bottle, etc. These designs should be produced in full-color 3-dimensional prototype form so that the design can be handled and even placed on a mock store shelf to evaluate for true context. Selecting the most compelling identities is necessary so that they can be checked legally, and in the case of international markets, culturally, as well as further adapted to the remaining applications. There may also be subtle refinements required, but essentially the design exploration is complete at this stage.

U.S. Registration Searches

At this stage we recommend taking the two solutions to your trusted trademark counsel to check for any potential registration mark conflicts in the United States. While it is not nearly as challenging to register a design as it is to trademark a name, we highly recommend conducting a thorough search to prevent any future lawsuits. Always go into the process with at least two designs. If one runs into problems, another solution may be the answer—better than paying a company major bucks to obtain legal rights. If both run into conflicts, additional refinements may be necessary to appease the law and registered mark owners.

Cultural Analysis

As with naming, it's important to run the designs by natives of the international markets the brand is intended to live in. Natives should evaluate for color, shape, and word appropriateness to ensure there are no negative, offensive, unintentional, or otherwise inappropriate meanings in the visual presentation of the brand identity. In the world of cultural and linguistic analysis, a neutral response to an identity is as good as gold. Meaning can always be built in—taking out negative meaning may be downright impossible.

International Registration Searches

As with names, it's essential to submit the proposed designs to international registration searches. The company Thomson and Thomson facilitates both name and design registration marks on a country-by-country basis. When retaining legal counsel, be sure your lawyers have substantial international trademark and intellectual property experience, as this interpretation and application process can be challenging for the best of lawyers.

Final Selections

Once all legal and cultural searches are completed, you should have one or two designs with which to begin adaptation to the various design applications. Or you may be back at some phase of creative exploration and/or refinement, in which case, take heart: it's happened to even the largest of companies as brands have proliferated in non-U.S. markets.

Adaptation

The adaptation phase extends the new look and feel to the business papers, brochures, signage, web sites, vehicles, products, etc. As each of the items are completed, the design team should present the client with the recommended applications for approval prior to preparation of final mechanicals. Here is a short list of the most common design applications a company will need to consider for adaptation of its new identity system:

- Business Cards
- Letterhead
- Second sheets
- Envelopes

- Faxes
- Invoices
- Transmittals
- Mailing labels
- Mailing envelopes
- Brochures
- Advertising
- Annual reports
- Web sites
- Signage
- Vehicles
- Uniforms
- Tradeshow booths
- Promotional items
- Product labels and boxes
- Shippers
- Point-of-purchase displays
- Product sell sheets

Mechanical Art

Mechanical artwork, or as it is sometimes called, final art, is similar to a blueprint in that a designer places the key elements (logomarks, tag lines, addresses, marketing copy, ingredients) in the correct position for printing or manufacturing. The technical requirements for mechanical art can include the actual finished size of the item (8½ × 11 for letterhead or 2 × 3½ for a business card), the number of colors and their specified codes (e.g., PMS185 red), the type of substrate, and other information like traps and bleeds. As recently as 1995, mechanical artwork was prepared on individual pieces of acetate and illustration board for each color. Sometimes these "boards" were huge, for large packages and cartons. Mechanical artwork is now prepared digitally and can be easily modified on the fly.

Design and Implementation Guidelines

Once the visual identity creation process is complete, a key tool to manage the identity in its use and implementation is to create a set of design standards or guidelines. Depending on the scope of the project and the types of resources your company has, the original external design team may do all of the implementation of your new identity system or hand off the adaptation and mechanical art work for an internal group to complete. This generally depends on resources, budget, and timing. For a smooth internal implementation and for the continuity of ongoing maintenance, we recommend the development of design guidelines. These documents can range from simple 10- to 15-page documents, to massive binder-based systems (we call them shelfware), to online digital databases. The guidelines can also combine visual with verbal identity guidelines. The scope will vary with the complexity of the identity program, size of the company, time, and resources. For most companies, there are a set of core guidelines that need to be clearly defined for designers (internal or external) and printers to refer to for consistent application of the new identity system. A complete summary of guideline sections is covered in Chapter 9.

5

IDENTITY MESSAGING

Messaging is a term that's been around for a long time, but like the terms *brand* and *branding*, these days it means a lot of different things to a lot of different folks. While messaging is automatically created for public relations and advertising campaigns, identity messaging is often ignored. Brand identity messaging is, essentially, all the components of the verbal identity after the top-level brand name. Think about what your identity says. How does it express itself verbally? What do the product, service, division, and subsidiary names communicate about the overall identity? What vocabulary is used to describe its core positioning, values, features, and benefits? How does this translate to building an image through advertising, public relations, and marketing? The messaging hierarchy moves from most proprietary to least proprietary and most general. In descending order of information, messaging consists of the nomenclature, the positioning tag line or parent company strap line, the audience messaging matrix, and copy points. Each layer adds a dimension to the entire brand identity, and ultimately to the image. Each layer brings the total identity to vibrant, tangible life.

Nomenclature Is Your Friend

The top level of messaging is nomenclature. It's the at-a-glance view of all company, subsidiary, division, product, service, technology, and any other branded names. From this vantage point you can see all the names that a company offers, the naming strategy and tone used, and the way the names are organized—by division, product, service, etc. One of the keys to nomenclature is consistency. A brand's nomenclature relates to messaging in that how clear, understandable, and relevant your company's brand names are signifies to internal and external (including financial) audiences what your company brand represents. It is another form of self-expression. A company will express itself succinctly and clearly or in quite the opposite manner.

Nomenclature options include the following links: corporate, linguistic, thematic, and hybrid. A *corporate link* consists of the corporate brand linked to all divisions, products, services, technologies, and acquisitions. (See Figure 5–1.) Subbrand names are either

Figure 5–1. FedEx company nomenclature. A color system is employed on the "Ex" portion of the visual identity to further distinguish such company identity. Purple is used in the rest of the identity to maintain consistent linkage of the identities and the back of its corporate color heritage. Reprinted with permission from FedEx Corporation.

generically descriptive or proprietary with an emphasis more on the former. Proprietary brands are linked back to the corporate brand as a part of its name or as an endorsement. The identities usually reflect the parent brand's visual identity.

Linguistic links include letters, acronyms, words, or word roots used as a linguistic device to link the division, product, service, or technology brand names to each other. This in turn allows for a unified, cohesive naming convention. Visual identities usually consist of the same logo, font, color treatments, or selected common elements applied consistently to each subbrand. (See Figure 5–2.)

A *thematic link* employs evocative words to name subbrands or branded elements of a web site in order

Big Mac
McSalad Shaker® Salads
Chicken McGrill
McFlurry
McCafe

Figure 5–2. Sample of McDonald's product nomenclature. Used with permission from McDonald's Corporation.

Figure 5–3. Sample of Yahoo! product/service nomenclature. Reprinted with permission of Yahoo!.

to link the names thematically back to the parent brand name. Visual identity makes use of selected common elements from the logo, typography, and colors consistently for each subbrand. Because of the difficulty in obtaining a trademark status for names, this option is seldom if ever employed exclusively. However, as with our Yahoo! example, it can be an effective and clever means of reinforcing the company brand name even when used sparingly. (See Figure 5–3.)

There are several types of *hybrid models* that combine the corporate, linguistic, and thematic links. We have detailed these as separate nomenclature options for educational purposes. They are in reality seldom used 100 percent. Even the most brand-conscious companies tend to have some kind of a hybrid system in place.

The real key to creating the best nomenclature practices lies in consistency, simplicity, brevity. These three golden words should be ingrained into the company's mantra.

1. *Consistently* create, apply, and enforce all brand names so that when all names are viewed as one nomenclature system, there are synergies between all names. The last thing a company wants is a few irreverent brand names here, a few traditional names there, and a lot of sup-posedly real descriptive English words that your own administrative assistant doesn't under-stand. If an irreverent tone is what is truly war-ranted by your positioning strategy, then make sure that this tone is applied to all names, not a few random ones.

2. Keep it *simple*. When you view all brand names as one nomenclature system, it becomes rather

obvious where long, extravagant names become a liability.

3. Keep it *brief*—especially when dealing with multiple brand relationships. Make sure that all brand names are short and to the point.

How the names are organized for internal and external audiences is equally important. It may seem obvious, but there are countless companies out there that list all the names of their products and services, but without any sort of organizational context. Now really, who wants to wade through a large list of proprietary brand names with no context about the nature of the offer and no context about how many other related choices the company may offer? We have worked with more than one large publicly traded company where a good percentage of the employees didn't know what products or services their own company offered when looking at a list of names. If your employees have a difficult time figuring out what your brand names stand for, you can be assured your potential customers will have an even harder time doing so.

Which leads us to the second part of the nomenclature equation: *organization*. No, we don't mean organization in the sense of, "Sure, my shoes are organized: I just shoved them all in the closet." We mean take the shoes, make sure they're in matched pairs, separate them into dressy, casual, sport, and other relevant categories. Place them neatly onto category-labeled shelves so that anyone can know at a glance not only where they're located but just how many different shoe options you have. Organization is as important to the company with a corporate-dominant and generic-descriptor branding model as it is to one with the corporate-invisible model. Viacom is a great example of a more or less corporate-invisible model, with many brands under the parent company. It does an excellent job of organizing its brands, considering the wide range of products, and especially ages of the intended audiences. Even an adolescent can understand all that the company offers. This organization extends from Viacom's marketing collateral to its web site. (See Figure 5–4.)

Positioning Tag Lines

Early on in the book we discussed what positioning tag lines are and how they differ from advertising tags. If you're still under the impression that a positioning tag line is a slogan, go back and review Chapter 1 thoroughly. We love positioning tag lines

Figure 5-4. Sample of Viacom-owned company nomenclature. Reprinted with permission from Viacom.

because while they may lack the sex appeal of a traditional advertising tag, they can go a long way in helping to establish a brand identity in the mind of consumers—the same consumers who have a gazillion other brand images thrown at them daily. Like nomenclature, it establishes an immediate context for the brand, and especially the brand name.

The art of creating a positioning tag line is to review the positioning strategy and in particular the positioning statement. The positioning tag line is essentially a bulleted version of the positioning statement. The tag line can be written in a straight-forward descriptive tone-for example, "McKesson-Empowering Healthcare"—or a slightly unusual and evocative tone-for example, "Amazon.com—Earth's Biggest Selection" or "FedEx—The World On Time."

The World On Time® is a registered service mark of Federal Express Corporation ("Fedex") and an example of a positioning tag line that spoke to the re-positioning of FedEx in 1994. (FedEx refers to The World On Time as a brand line.) Our friend and colleague Dave Hurlbert penned the tag as a member of the Landor team responsible for concepting the new positioning, creating the positioning tag line and visual identity, and implementing the new identity. After extensive strategy development, it was determined that the features and benefits of time-definite delivery, along with global service, were crucial to articulate in the tag line. Another key objective was to say all of this in as few words as possible. The resulting tag line achieved these objectives so successfully, it appears on everything from packaging to trucks to the title of a FedEx management book written in 1996 by James C. Wetherbe.

If you think a tag line is created over a pizza-and-beer lunch, think again. Several tag lines, and in some cases hundreds, are created to identify the right ones. In the case of The World On Time, there were over 200 other tag lines created over the course of two full-time weeks. Like names, tag lines are created based on a creative brief that employs all the same positioning strategy information as the naming and design briefs, as well as applicable technical parameters and of course preliminary creative directions. While no one tag line can be equally effective for all target audiences, it should speak clearly to the audiences that are most important to your business. Like any creative process, range is important to explore as some of the most unexpected yet highly appropriate solutions can magically appear. Putting too many constraints on creative directions and tone is like telling an artist to paint with one color.

The classic positioning tag line is usually something like:

Newco—The Leading Insert-What-We-Do-Here Company

We do believe, however, that a balance of descriptive and evocative tones is what best serves a positioning tag line. (Refer back to The World On Time example.) When managing or creating your own tag line, do avoid words like "leading," "leader," "preeminent," and "premier." Yes, we've been guilty of using these words as well, but we realize the error of our ways and now avoid these words at all costs. Remember: unique, ownable, and defendable—not what every other company uses and expects to hear.

If you want to prevent others from using a similar tag line, then you must register it as a servicemark in the United States. The same trademark counsel who conducted your name trademark searches and registration can conduct a domestic servicemark search to check for availability in the United States and then register the servicemark. While servicemarks are not nearly as tough to register as a trademarked name, it's wise to screen carefully and go into the process with at least four to five tag line candidates, lest legal obstructions prevent the line of choice from becoming legally yours. Keep in mind that, as with all registered marks, if you choose to use marks that are too close to an existing registered mark, you can be sued for a great deal of money by the registered owner.

Cultural and linguistic issues are another reason for choosing more than a couple of tag lines. As we all know, what communicates well in this country can be an international tragedy when exported to even one of our neighbors. (Golden Guideline No. 1 of global brand identity: Do your homework lest you become another Nova or Pajero story.) Tag lines must, must—we repeat—must be checked by native speakers and residents for cultural and linguistic appropriateness, as they exist both in English and in translation. Some countries require that a tag line be translated for registration purposes. Which brings us to Golden Guideline No. 2: Nothing means the same thing to everyone. Even global brands like Coke and McDonald's have not found a tag line or slogan that can work all over the world both in English and in translation. Have multiple tag lines for multiple markets. Whether the tag is more appropriate in English or in translation is dependent on target audiences and target markets. Be sure to get plenty of local linguistic and legal guidance per market.

Parent Company Strap Lines

Strap lines are related to tag lines. These are the parent company endorsements that appear in small print underneath the brand: for example, "UUNet, A WorldCom Company." Strap lines generally appear for legal reasons and can be modified slightly for marketing purposes. Basic word "components" of the legalese must remain the same, such as the name of the parent company and whether the subbrand being identified is a company, subsidiary, or division. The words in between, so to speak, can change slightly.

"A Subsidiary of XYZ" can be changed for marketing purposes to "Another Proud Subsidiary of XYZ." Variations of the strap line can overlap with the tag line; one line effectively positions the company, subsidiary, division, or even product or service with target audiences while communicating the relationship of the parent company. This is generally most effective when establishing parent company relationships with subbrands that stand alone. For instance when deciding what words to actually use, be it the basic or embellished versions, the key is first to base the solutions on your strategy and second to ensure that the strap line is used consistently regardless of medium. Target audiences will receive a consistent message of the parent and subbrand relationship, and your legal team will be grateful if and when they have to defend or prosecute use, servicemark, or trademark issues in court. As with the tag line, be sure to get your legal team's approval on using any version of a strap line as well as linguistic and cultural guidance for foreign markets and nonnative languages.

Audience Messaging Matrix

As we discussed in Chapter 2, an audience messaging matrix is a tool that matches target audiences to key message points, which most often are features and benefits. The resulting hierarchy of communication presents key information in the order most relevant to your primary and secondary audiences. The matrix adds an invaluable level of specificity to the overall identity messaging that can then be directly applied to a number of applications such as sales sheets, direct marketing, press releases, or even analyst and shareholder information. The finished matrix can also be helpful in identifying what's missing from either a product and service perspective, a marketing perspective, or both. The process of creating an audience messaging matrix is straightforward but does require diligence and, to be most effective, validation.

To begin creating a matrix, gather together a team that includes those responsible for short- and long-term business strategy, marketing, and sales. Make a list of your brand's primary and secondary target customers and influencers. This can be done by industry or sector and by division or title. Once the entire list is compiled, rank order each primary audience of target customers, then go on to the secondary audiences of influencers. Influencers can be prioritized by general rank and in individual descending order.

The example that follows was created for a database client based in Europe. The matrix was created beginning with areas of responsibilities and corresponding titles by the company's president and senior marketing executives, who then took the information to sales for further refinement. The titles were chosen based on the people the company's sales team would speak with directly (be it influencer or decision maker) as well as those who would ultimately make the decision about purchasing the intended products and services.

For a broader overview, we recommend listing profiles of companies by industry or sector that are broken down further by company size or sales revenue. Then go on to specific areas of responsibility and titles. This will paint a larger picture of your company's target audience.

In the example that follows the primary audiences are listed by corporate area and title. They are listed numerically to indicate priority. The secondary audiences are more general and listed by level of influence—A, B, or C.

Primary Audiences: Target Customers
1. Corporate Finance: CFO, controller and below
2. Corporate Legal
3. Information Technology: MIS/CIO/CTO
4. Sales/Marketing: VP/director/manager
5. Human Resources: VP/director

Secondary Audiences: Influencers
A. Industry analysts (influences executive "C" level)
A. Press—trade (influences field)
A. Partners: Big 5 (influences "C" level)
B. Partners: Big 5 (influences field)
B. Executive management "C" level: CEO/COO/CMO
B. Press business (influences corporation)
C. Investors: individual/corporation
C. Corporate communications: VP/director

Once the primary and secondary audiences are in place and prioritized, go back to your list of features and benefits that were created during the positioning strategy. Review the list to ensure that all features and benefits are also prioritized. We also recommend noting which feature or benefit is unique and differentiated from the competition. Rank-ordered benefits generally correspond to the equivalent rank-ordered feature. Features can and usually do have more than one benefit.

Here is a partial list of the prioritized features and benefits for our database company's platform of products and services. As discussed in Chapter 2, it's important to note that these were prioritized as a part of the overall identity positioning strategy based on general audiences. Prioritization based on specific audiences is where the matrix goes to work.

Features	Benefits
1. Flexible modeling*	1. Control of decentral- ized operations
2. Tight Excel integration	2. Improved collaboration
3. Statutory consolidation*	3. Integrate internal- external financials
4. Web enablement	4. Remote access
5. Multiplatform support	5. No installation
6. End user modeling	6. Runs anyplace, anywhere
7. Short training time	7. Low IT involvement
8. Real-time calculations	8. Intuitive
9. Speed and ease of deployment	9. Short training time
10. Certified integration with data warehouses*	10. Localized services*

* Indicates feature or benefit differentiated from competition

Forming the Matrix

Now that the individual components are in place, it's time to start forming the actual audience-specific matrix. With your audience and features and benefits lists in hand, begin at the top and ask yourself the following questions:

- Who is your number one target audience?
- What do individuals in that particular industry or sector need to know about your company, platform, product, or service that is most relevant to them?
- What are the top three to five features and benefits that apply most to that individual's need?

Answering these questions with a team who represent a cross-section of the company (such as short- and long-term business strategy, sales, and marketing) is critical for this process. Equally critical is appointing an objective facilitator who can obtain this information from all team members and facilitate the rank-order placement of each component of the matrix. This information can come from in-house knowledge, sales tracking, previous research studies, or newly commissioned quantitative or qualitative research. We often recommend a combination approach, starting with on-hand information and then validating with research once a first pass is completed on the matrix. If little is available, this is an appropriate time to commission research, first to obtain the core information and then form the matrix based on the results. In this case, validation can be followed up either directly with customers or through further research.

Our example matrix begins with the number one primary audience and then states what the audience's general need is that the platform of products and services can fill. Next, features and benefits (asterisks denote those not offered by competitors) are listed and prioritized based on the audience and key needs. This process is repeated for each target audience, including each of the influencers.

Target Audience: Corporate Finance, HQ: CFO, controller and below

Needs: Reliable information, readily accessible, relevant, collaboration

Features

1. Flexible modeling*
2. Statutory consolidation framework*
3. Real-time calculation
4. Certified integration*

Benefits

1. Improved collaboration
2. Integrate internal-external financials
3. Localized services*
4. Low IT involvement

Target Audience: IT

Needs: Control and dissemination of data

Features

1. Certified integration with data warehouses*
2. Web enablement
3. Multiplatform support
4. End-user modeling

Benefits

1. Control of decentralized operations
2. Runs anyplace, anywhere
3. Integrate internal-external financials
4. Low IT involvement

Your matrix may be limited to the top three to five features and benefits or can be expanded to all applicable features and benefits. Comprehensive lists are beneficial when accompanied by an abbreviated "executive version" for quick reference. Doing so ensures that the entire company knows and uses the same type of language regardless of application. They're also extremely helpful as an official reference guide for outside media agencies or consultants.

Creating Copy Points

Every copywriter has a different style of creating copy for marketing materials, web sites, etc. Some are outline enthusiasts and others prefer just the facts combined with the freedom to explore concepts and tone. What all copywriters need to create copy that ties in well with the brand are *copy points*—bullet points of information about the overall brand, the offer, and the target audience.

Copy points are derived largely from a brand's positioning strategy and audience messaging matrix. From a copywriter's perspective, the more detailed information you can give about what is to be marketed, the better. Refer back to your original positioning strategy—the proposition, price points, target markets, relevant corporate relationships, communication attributes, core essence, positioning strategy—and your newly created audience messaging matrix. There you will find all the factual ingredients necessary to write the copy.

Once the brand positioning information is established, the remaining copy points consist of the exact context (such as the services page of the brand's web site or a direct-mail letter and brochure for new customers), parameters around promotions, sales, and general tone.

Tone is another area derived directly from the positioning strategy, and especially the communication attributes. If a brand's attributes are casual and approachable, the last thing you want is an institutional and rigid tone. Of course, there is room in between to interpret tone. Depicting a picture of your brand as an actual person fleshed out with physical and personality traits, habits, etc., can strongly assist in visualizing your brand interacting with an intended customer. Remember our Joe Jones example in Chapter 2?

Joe Jones has dark curly hair and blue eyes. He's 6′2″, with a thin build. He's a tech writer, lives in a loft in the Mission district of San Francisco, drives a brand new silver Z3, gives regularly to the local homeless shelter, and hires a cleaner once a week to clean up his messes. What would he say to his number one target customer? How would that differ from his last-priority influencer? How would he present himself both physically and verbally? Is he soft-spoken or gregarious? Is his vocabulary based on advanced English classes at Purdue or episodes of *Friends*? Creating a specific persona can open up a range of tone and vocabulary while still being directly related to the brand positioning. Most copywriters will appreciate the tangible image, and the end result is copy that is a coherent extension of your brand.

6

DIGITAL
IDENTITY

Not so many years ago, large companies were blinded by the Internet headlights. They simply didn't know what to do with the new-fangled medium. While the start-ups got it and quickly created identities that have even more rapidly faded from memory (I remember the gerbil shot out of the cannon, but who was the company again?), big firms had nary a clue. Fast-forward a couple of years and, my, how the pendulum has swung.

The Dawning of a New Age

When the Internet first came into being, many established companies viewed it as some terrible alien beast that had to be tamed in order to ride its power. In 1994, Alycia Perry attended a conference in Scottsdale, Arizona, about marketing for the Internet. The concept was so new at that time that strategies such as sending promotional coupons as e-mails were still considered avant-garde. Sponsor-created television content (especially in TV's early days) as a time-honored model for web content to emulate was the revelation to everyone seeking a guiding light (no soap opera pun intended). Alycia grew up with computers and understood the power of a web site. During the early 1990s, she created the Bosnia Help Page as a political, cultural, and humanitarian resource for those interested in the civil war that raged in that part of the world at the time. With no HTML experience and minimal design skills, she created a site that was readable, aesthetically appealing, and compelling. Agencies in Washington, D.C., jumped at the chance to be included, and ordinary citizens around the world used it to get informed and involved in humanitarian efforts. Now translate this successful microcosm to a commercial web site—isn't that what all companies desire? Sponsors eager to be included in the site and investors and customers motivated to take action? We knew early on that the Internet was a phenomenal marketing force.

The fear many established companies exhibited was laughable and really very baffling. Why wouldn't a company want to harness the power of a medium that reached global audiences instantly? No, there were not many Internet users at the time, but the ones that were out there were willing, eager, and affluent. Some companies viewed the medium with great reverence and fear. Some made tentative efforts, posting their corporate brochure on the web (a.k.a. brochureware). But others, mostly GenX renegades, dove in fearlessly.

The brands that emerged as the web's champions were brands that had never been heard of before. We all know that Netscape (née Mosaic), AOL, and Yahoo! achieved near-immediate brand recognition, but the branding trends that emerged as a result of these successes were both awe-inspiring and beyond sublime.

Early users and observers of the Internet could see that things were going to be approached differently in every aspect of the medium. In its early days, Alycia led the program to name a new online dating service that was put out by a national financial services company. The process was tedious, but with all the team members finally on board and in synch, they chose a name that was quick, catchy, even a little hip, and not the least bit related to its parent company. The pilot program never did quite make it to its online debut, but the lesson served its purpose: even mature, experienced, marketing execs were catching on to the fact that they needed an identity that was different.

The Dot-Com Dance

It was the young, however, who faced the new frontier in a radically different way. The disappointing reality was that brand identities applied to the digital age were simply rehashed versions of a few early dot-com success stories. As the 1990s marched on, suddenly *everyone* wanted to be different, and the more the better. The word "differentiated" dominated the marketing buzz. Amazon was perhaps the greatest poster child of naming. It was hip, cool, unexpected as a name. And it seemed nearly everyone was in hot pursuit of an equally exotic and unexpected name. Earlier in the 1990s, Alycia and our namers routinely searched dictionaries for unusual, exotic words. Usually the presentation of such a word as a preferred name recommendation was received with an arched eyebrow at best. Suddenly these names were flying out of the dictionary and into the U.S. trademark office. But we're getting ahead of ourselves.

It really all started with the original trend of adding the .com suffix to the official brand name, signifying an online presence and also serving as a useful mnemonic device to remind people of the new URL address format. It seemed no company could be a dot-com and not have a .com in its name. If it did not, it may have been—dare we say it—not a pure-play dot-com. Adding "online" to the name was the other way of signifying that the brand was found on the web. Then came the plethora of e- brands (eBay) and eventually i- brands (iVillage). There was even a brief b- phase (bCentral). The shortcomings of these names were obvious: the more .com, e-, and i- names appeared, the more dilution there was in the actual strength of the name, and therefore the memorability by the target customer or audience. For those who started out as pure-play dot-coms and then went into other sales and distribution channels such as catalogue, telephone, brick-and-mortar environments, their Internet-based prefixes and suffixes severely limited the elasticity of the brand name, often becoming a liability. This was particularly true for those exercising last-ditch efforts to adopt different business models. What may have been different because of an e- was no longer relevant as the companies offered products and services through traditional channels.

Then of course there was the generic word craze. The trend peaked when Business.com sold for $7.5 million dollars to the highest bidder. The generic word craze was an interesting point in trademark history. Initially Wine.com, the purveyor of wines to the average Joe online, was accepted as a registrable name. While "wine" qualified as a common and generic word (and therefore not registrable), the .com suffix was deemed unique and fanciful enough as a modifier. Therefore Wine.com could be registered as a trademark. But as the trend of marrying a generic name with a .com modifier came to a frenzied peak, the U.S. Trademark Office changed the rules and refused to register on the Principal Register all such names as merely descriptive and not registrable. The purpose of going through the trademark process to begin with is to strengthen rights in the mark, especially against competitors. If competitors select a name that comes a little too close to your registered mark, you can stop them more easily with a registration and even ask for damages. The new position of the U.S. Trademark Office made the .com marks much weaker. Therefore, Wine.com could not stop competitors from using very similar marks, including eWines, iWines, and Wines On-line. The companies could cannibalize one another. It was not a wise move. And today most are out of business. (Wines.com was saved through acquisition by e-Vineyards.) Again Dr. John Nash's equilibrium theory was applied to brands: If you all go after the same thing (especially in the same way), each brand can and likely will block another, leading to the demise of most of the companies.

At one point the naming process for dot-coms became so surreal that it seemed all marketing taboos had been systematically broken and nothing was too outrageous in the pursuit of cool. Where previously names had been conservative (think Altria and Lucent), the quest for the next Amazon and Yahoo! was then in overdrive. Quokka.com, FogDog, Fatbrain, Kozmo.com, and others became the new poster children of what a successful name should look and sound like.

The irreverent differentiation in naming translated to the rest of the brand identity. Years earlier IBM set the precedent in traditional business identities with its use of the color blue. As a result blue, conservative identities became synonymous with mature, traditional, and global companies. Big, chunky, clean-lined identities with serif fonts also dominated the traditional set. As a 180-degree reaction to brick-and-mortar companies, dot-com visual identities sported colors such as safety orange, green, and purple to stand out from the blue on-lookers. The shapes used in identities became more organic, sensual, fluid, and free-form. Serif fonts, such as the one you see printed in this book, were replaced by the clean-edged look of sans serif fonts. Because of the Internet's screen-based format, the print medium was often ignored. Size and scalability were flat-out forgotten. Consequently, what looked good on a computer screen often lost its impact in print ads, marketing and sales brochures, small black-and-white newspaper print, or billboards lining Highway 101 from San Francisco to Silicon Valley. We even remember seeing some dot-com identities reproduced for investment journals that were all together illegible. Experiential identities—specifically the web sites themselves—were hot to ooze-cool, making ever increasing use of animation, sound, and movie clips to keep a clear distance from the static corporate brochure look. In an effort to appear more substantial and increase perceived customer value, portals displayed greater amounts of text. As a direct result, the ubiquitous sans serif fonts were scaled down significantly to accommodate the volume of material. Viewing text from a PowerBook was at times a challenge, even for young eyes. It seemed that no matter what the purpose was of the site and company, the same look prevailed—and, sadly, this is still the case.

As our colleague Jeffrey Marcus noted, the standard for the dot-com identity was the name.com in sans serif type with a red-orange elipse supported by a tiny sans serif font and an overkill of Flash. The identity connoted global, cutting-edge, innovation, forward-thinking. Of course, dozens of companies had more or less the same identity, with the same cookie-cutter rationale. There was no denying that what started out as a movement to boldly explore the new frontier became little more than an exercise in redundancy.

We have painted a rather gloomy overview of what was in order to illustrate predominant practices of the time and what can be avoided in the future. There has been much discussion and debate since the year 2000 about what happened in the dot-com and tech sectors and why the bubble burst. We tend to concur with other writers and consultants who have studied best and worst of practices of the time: failure came in large part because young, ambitious, but inexperienced people thrust into executive roles. While many were highly intelligent, the investors' shortsightedness, the executive staffs' inexperience, and everyone's overwhelming desire to ride the money wave and ignore the existing system was fatal. Brand fundamentals were thrown out the window and replaced with highly irreverent and highly irrelevant advertising. This quest to be different, while ignoring the brand's relevance to audiences, sealed the coffin.

The Simple Truth about Digital Identities

So how does one approach a digital identity? The first guideline to remember is the most basic of all: The Internet is yet another marketing and distribution channel. Simple, yes, but fundamental. This is true of both business-to-consumer (B2C) and business-to-business (B2B) plays. Land's End, for instance, uses its web site in the same way as it uses its print catalogue: as a marketing and distribution channel to display its clothes to families across the country. This is the same consumer model for all types of businesses, ranging from financial services to health services. Inktomi develops and markets network infrastructure applications for network service providers and enterprises. In plain speak, it offers things that make the

Internet and networks work more efficiently for businesses—a classic B2B offer spun for the technology age. Although it's a far cry from retailing basic cotton turtlenecks and tote bags to folks in Minnesota—Inktomi's site is like Land's End: another point of contact for potential sales and limited distribution channel. But in this case it's IT gurus for Fortune 1000 companies who are the target customers.

In addition to consumer versus business, there is technology branding—the technology version of ingredient branding (more on ingredient and other types of nontraditional branding in Chapter 7). Microsoft.Net Passport is a web-based technology that enables computers to talk to each other quickly by sending user information such as user names and passwords to web sites. The end benefit is the web user inputs less information, thereby saving time. Microsoft.Net Passport is marketed to kids, adults, and enterprises as a web technology that is beneficial to each audience. This is a technology that would traditionally be invisible to end users as a branded entity. But because the technology is branded as Microsoft.Net Passport and visible to distinct audiences, the identity and service enhances and reinforces messaging of the overall Microsoft brand (although some may argue whether the messaging is actual or aspirational). The real importance is not so much the ingredient brand as it is the halo effect it gives to Microsoft as a whole. Microsoft.Net Passport is convenient, efficient, and ubiquitous, as is the overall brand and its other products and services. Again, this technology (ingredient) brand is an example of another marketing and distribution channel—in this case, indirectly for other Microsoft products and services.

We offer this fundamental review not to trivialize all web sites but rather to illustrate that among the different types of companies with a web presence, the basics of brand identity remain the same. There is no need to treat the Internet as something outside the norm of marketing—it's one of its basic vehicles. Therefore, brand identity development for an Internet-based company, and development for a traditional company with an Internet presence, follow highly similar practices. We believe that the main difference in approach and philosophy comes from the distinction between completely new brands and reinvented ones, not between a dot-com and a brick-and-mortar company, as was done in the late 1990s.

If a brand is to be primarily web-based, it follows the same strategy guidelines as established in Chapter 2. The web-oriented aspects that make the new brand unique, as compared to say a retail-based brand, should be contained in the key features and benefits and positioning statement and reflected in the communication attributes. Thus, the strategy will influence and guide the creative development of a name, a visual identity, and messaging in the same manner as any other brand.

Rather than use the dot-com predecessor strategy of NewName.com or e-NewName, develop a stand-alone name that has an appropriate descriptor or positioning tag line that reflects the brand's web base. Let's take a real-time news service as an example: Alpha (name) Real-Time News (generic descriptor), Global Information Downloaded (positioning tag line). The verbal identity is considerably longer than, say, Alpha.com or e-Alpha alone, but it sets the stage for growth. If Alpha decides to expand into other channels or business lines such as print magazines and television shows, the company name can remain the same and the generic descriptor and positioning tag line can be changed to accommodate each new channel or line. If the overall name is Alpha, then a corporate-dominant (single-brand) strategy is created using the .com as one of several descriptors.

- Alpha Inc.
- Alpha.com
- Alpha radio

- Alpha TV
- Alpha business journals

Considering the amount of time, money, and commitment necessary to create, register, and enforce a name, it's far more efficient and simple to create a new descriptor or positioning tag line than a new name.

A logomark or wordmark would be developed to be appropriate for *all* channels, with application modifications made to accommodate the different mediums, for example appropriate colors, size, and scale for television screens to print media to web-enabled cell phones.

Computer monitors and televisions reproduce color in a red/green/blue (RGB) format. RGB can produce 16 million colors, more than the human eye can detect. But desktop and commercial printers print colors in cyan/magenta/yellow/black (CMYK), or process color. As a result, what you see on the computer monitor may not resemble what you print and most likely will look different from monitor to monitor. Several effects come together to cause this problem:

- Monitors and output devices have limitations. Each device has a range of colors it can reproduce, called its color gamut. These vary with the type and model. The printer type, ink, and paper quality, and the condition of the printer also affect the results. Equipment can easily be miscalibrated, and very expensive, specialized accessories are required to keep it to a predictable standard. Printers that dither can only create a limited number of colors. If you attempt to print a color that does not fall within its abilities, it will produce the nearest match. The printer's resolution is important to its dithering ability, so higher-resolution printers usually print higher-quality color.

As a general rule, the more application mediums the identity lives in, the simpler the use of color, shape, and form should be. There are various international standards that can be selected: SWOP, TOYO, DIC, Euroscale, CIELAB, CIELUV, Pantone, Hexachrome. And of course there are custom colors, which need to be converted to RGB, CMYK, spot color, and so on, depending on the application. We recommend the Pantone system, which offers thousands of colors in a format that is internationally accepted. The colors you select for your identity system will not only act as a mnemonic device for recognition and recall but aid in setting the character and personality. (For more information on the Pantone system, go to www.pantone.com. Their site also has a lot of rich information on color theory.)

Digital Identity Musts

Whether the brand is new or reinvented, your strategy, verbal identity, and visual identity should be well defined, relevant, and, hopefully, differentiated. The digital identity begins at the point of applying this well-defined brand identity to your web site, or for that matter any other form of interactive mediums. In other words, it is the beginning of the experience, or experiential identity. The combined verbal and visual identity should be applied consistently throughout the site and displayed prominently. It should be sized and scaled appropriately, making it clear and legible. The colors should translate from CMYK (print) to RGB (monitor) and vice versa. The identity should translate from a computer screen to a PDA screen to a wireless cell phone screen. The printed version from an end user's laser printer should look just as good in gray scale, color, and the original screen identity. The identity shouldn't be buried somewhere on the page—it should be immediately accessible, recognizable, and in the same place every time. And of course the site should be readable with all browsers and sizes of computers (for example, with a 19-inch PC-compatible screen and an Apple PowerBook). There should be a consistent overall look and feel within the site as well as with the brand in all mediums (print, TV, radio, retail location, etc.).

Believe it or not, there are still commercial sites that do not feature their brand identity throughout. Some even adopt the "no logo" strategy. Agnes B., the French clothier, is an example of an artistic site with a lack of consistent brand placement. Featuring your brand identity throughout the site is a must on every page, not only to leverage every possible moment to reinforce brand recognition but to ensure that if users go away from the site and then hit the history button, they will know that a particular page belongs to Brand X. Think about branding's original purpose: If a cow wandered away, anyone could tell where it came from by the brand. We'd also like to make the case that consistently applying the brand identity is true for nearly any interactive medium—whether it's a PDA screen, a cell phone interface, a hand-held device, or a kiosk or screen of any kind. The trend in television to brand the bottom of the screen with the station name, while annoying to some, is in our view a brilliant move. With hundreds of channels to choose from these days, viewers know instantly which network they're watching and have a much greater chance of remembering the network's name and visual identity.

Variations of brand treatments among mediums can occur selectively. Sometimes there is room to create a slightly different treatment of an identity for interactive mediums (Internet, PDAs, wireless, etc.). Or perhaps it is for a very specific target audience with highly different needs and aesthetic tastes, such as kids or teens, for one or all channels. We urge caution in following this path. Slightly different treatments can provide an interesting visual system but can also fragment the brand, thereby reducing memorability. These tend to work best with older, established brands such as Visa or FedEx—in other words, brands that are etched in consumers' minds and have room to expand their identities online. This must be well thought out and enforced consistently. Enforcement is key; otherwise the online identity may bleed over to internal pet projects or, heaven forbid, other unsanctioned external uses. In addition to competing identities with or without brand police enforcement, the other danger is the possibility of no or little synergy between the online and offline visual and experiential identities. This approach takes foresight, planning, and applications, and brand police to enforce where and how the treatments are applied.

Creating the Experience

With these givens, the specific details of how the combined verbal and visual are applied are dependent on the experience desired. The more the experience comes alive through relevancy, the more target consumers and audiences and advertisers will want to engage fully with the branded site. For a web site, prioritize the top five reasons why any given target audience would come to your site. What are they looking for? What are they seeking to accomplish? Repeat this exercise for all target audiences. Now look at the results. What are the common threads? Now expand this to all points of contact. How is the online experience different from the brick-and-mortar experience different from the telephone experience? What are the synergies? What differentiates each? The results of this exploration, combined with your positioning strategy, may provide inspiration for a different way to lay out the user interface, and particularly the navigation bars. It may even provide new graphic layouts and vehicles for advertisers. (If you successfully manage to accomplish this, call us.) The architecture and navigation of the site must be relevant to these audiences and their needs to make the experience rewarding and engaging. In an age of little time and too much information, efficiency is key. There is little room for redundancy or for buried navigation links critical to those users.

In terms of messaging and content, the more engaging and relevant the better. Create a copy tone and style that is unique to the online presence rather than mimicking a corporate brochure or sales sheet verbatim. Going back to the messaging matrix, ensure all points are covered for all applicable audiences and in a way that is not buried or lost in the site. There are those customers who shop online for the convenience or search for information with few frills and those who explore for the sport of it, hoping to find something new and engaging. These could be Chief Technical Officers or stay-at-home dads. There are people who want a multidimensional experience and those who want just the facts, preferably as quickly as possible. The real challenge is providing information and exchanges with options for both. The basic information with or without frills must be presented in a manner that is relevant and efficient. There is nothing more aggravating than searching for need-to-know information that is buried five or more pages into a site. In the case of an online product or service, how easy is it to find out information about the offering, ask questions, make the transaction, and follow up as needed with tech or customer support? In other words, is the information easily accessible via the site or other support channels? Regardless of approach, the experience needs to be quick, easy, and pleasurable enough that the user wants to do it again.

The journey to obtain information doesn't necessarily have to be business-as-usual serious. As those stupid-grin inducing ad campaigns remind us through the years, have fun with designing the experience, and yes, we even mean that for B2B plays as well. Is there something pleasurable and engaging to interact with on the site? Seek innovative ways to entice someone to come back. Are there added-value propositions unique to the web, such as Internet-only fares, specials, or coupons? Is there a unique visual or auditory experience that is consistent with the brand and objectives of the site? Or is there so much Flash that it's a distraction to the experience? Needless to say, efficient options to disengage extra effects such as sound, animation, and video clips when desired are required fare. Pleasure beats agony any day.

What Endures

The intent of this chapter is to explore issues and best and worst practices to consider when creating a new identity for Internet usage and emerging interactive mediums. We could go into much detail about current examples, but the rapid pace of technological changes makes this exercise futile. Take the history, the mistakes, the lessons learned; take the guidelines and questions and apply them to the sites and interfaces you encounter every day. Apply them to your own. No matter how technology changes, the basic tenets of relevancy, efficiency, and pleasurable experiences for different target audiences remain the same. This is what creates impact.

7

INGREDIENT BRANDING, TECHNOLOGY BRANDING, AND OTHER INTERESTING FORMULAS

In the last half of the last century, some unusual twists on brand creation took place. It was brought about by something widely referred to as *ingredient branding*—the creation of a brand for something proprietary that goes inside yet another product. Ingredient branding started as just that: patented or proprietary ingredients that were created as an "input" into other products, such as the now famous NutraSweet. To create more perceived value for the company, a brand for the input was created and backed by consistent application and heavy advertising. It was a way for consumer goods to transform the perception of a commodity into something unique and of value, therefore increasing consumer demand.

What would a stereo be without Dolby? How functional is a ski parka without Gore-Tex? Can you really cook something in the frying pan without Teflon? It's hard to believe that the branding phenomenon of NutraSweet, discovered accidentally by a researcher at G. D. Searle, would spur a whole new movement of branding applied to technology ingredients, turning a well-respected little company called Intel into one of the top consumer-recognized brands in the world.

As you may have guessed, creating an identity for an ingredient brand is not terribly different than for any other type of brand. What differs is reflected in the positioning strategy, naming, and visual objectives, and especially in the technical parameters. Types and sizes of applications (such as on computer chips, cell phone screens, or packaging that is dominated by the primary product brand) are usually very constrained in the case of ingredient brands. Therefore, size of the total brand identity matters more.

Once the identity is created, it's really brand-building efforts, and in particular co-op advertising, that makes building an ingredient brand unique. It's important to know when there are unique opportunities to create a brand. While this chapter cites many food, consumer good, and technology examples, these same opportunities can potentially be applied to proprietary services as well.

The Original Ingredient Brand

NutraSweet brand sweetener was discovered in 1965 by researcher James Schlatter while he was working with amino acids to develop a treatment for ulcers. When he licked his finger to pick up a piece of paper, he got his—and the world's—first taste of aspartame, a product 200 times sweeter than sugar and with very few calories. Soon after it was named NutraSweet and became the brand that revolutionized synthetic sweeteners for individuals and the food and beverage industries.

Aspartame underwent many years of testing, and was finally approved for consumer use in 1979 in France, where the product was marketed as "Canderel." The Canderel name is a combination of the words *candy* and *airelle,* the French word for wild cherry. Contrary to the "candy" implication, it was marketed only to pharmaceuticals and came in the form of a white tablet. Advertising the product was not permitted. However, the product gained recognition through the support of pharmacists and doctors who lauded the health benefits of the low-calorie sweetener. By the early 1980s, Canderel was marketed in much of Europe.[1]

By 1981, the U.S. Food and Drug Administration approved the tabletop use of NutraSweet. One year and nearly $80 million in start-up costs later, Equal was launched in the United States—right around the same time as NutraSweet. This helped create brand awareness for Equal, which quickly became recognized and accepted in the U.S. market. At that time, the U.S. tabletop sweetener market totaled about $110 million and was dominated by the saccharin-based product Sweet-N Low made by the Cumberland Packing Company. Although it was about three times more expensive than Sweet-N Low, Equal was an immediate market success.[2]

When the FDA approved aspartame for wet use, NutraSweet was offered to food and beverage manufacturers. The offer was backed by extensive advertising (estimated at $30 million annually) of the brand name aimed directly at end users and by cooperative advertising with manufacturers. The company gave discounts of up to 40 percent off the list price of aspartame to manufacturers who agreed to use 100 percent aspartame as a sweetener (versus aspartame and saccharin blends). The second half of the deal was to make NutraSweet their exclusive worldwide supplier and to display the NutraSweet trademark and distinctive red-and-white-swirl logo on their products and in their own advertising. Coca-Cola and Pepsi were the top brands to adapt their diet drink formulas with NutraSweet. Aspartame replaced virtually all the U.S. soft drink use of saccharin within two years of its introduction.[3]

Today, the company is the world's number one producer of the artificial sweetener aspartame. It sells its NutraSweet brand aspartame to makers of food, beverages, and tabletop sweeteners in more than 100 countries. In all, NutraSweet is used in some 5,000 products.[4] While aspartame has been under constant scrutiny over the years by the FDA, doctors, researchers, and health advocates, the NutraSweet brand remains strong. The brand's identity, marketing, and advertising practices have inspired many industries in how to create and build something that traditionally would have been invisible to end users and consumers.

Co-branding and Ingredients

The idea of creating a unique brand has always been about the transformation from commodity to something of value. Anyone can get bananas anywhere. A banana is a banana, right? But isn't it nice when a consumer requests Chiquita bananas each time she goes to purchase them at the store? Chiquita's accountants certainly think so. Turning the commodity into a unique brand to be sold on its own is the very origin of branding practices. What has come about in more recent times is the practice of turning a product brand that more or less identifies a commodity into an ingredient brand. Frito-Lay's Rold Gold pretzels flavored with Land O'Lakes butter, Oscar Mayer Lunchables with Kool-Aid drink included, Dreyer's Snickers ice cream, Ford Explorer Eddie Bauer Edition are among a handful of examples. While many of these examples can technically be classified as co-branded line extensions, they all have the same common denominator: One brand represents the product; the other brand represents the "ingredient" that makes this particular product unique both to other competitive brands and to sister brands within its own product family. This is the difference between the Ford Explorer XLS and the Ford Explorer Eddie Bauer Edition, for example.

Oscar Mayer Lunchables is a unique product line of prepared "lunch boxes" marketed to kids and busy moms that allows Kraft (Oscar Mayer's parent company) to market and sell primarily its own products, including (big surprise) Kool-Aid. While the Lunchables family do have official names to indicate package differences (including Oscar Mayer Lunchables Reduced Fat, Oscar Mayer All-Star Lunch Combinations, and Oscar Mayer Fun Snacks, among others), the brand relies on the visual effect of a transparent window to showcase all the ingredients. Thus, every branded product in the package differentiates and sells that particular Lunchable. Using such a strategy can breathe life into tired brands by adding a branded twist, usually marketed to younger, brand-savvy audiences.

Through its successful marriage with Eddie Bauer, Ford found a unique formula for adding value to its Ford Explorer line and appealing to brand-conscious parents. As of the summer of 1999, 1 million signed leather-seat Ford Explorer Eddie Bauer Editions were on the roads.

Eddie Bauer has made its signature style a valuable ingredient and asset to other brands while building its own. From diaper bags to SUVs to eyeware, Eddie Bauer is a licensing power house. In addition to its licensed partnership with Ford, it has licensed its style ingredient to the Lane furniture maker to create the Eddie Bauer Lifestyles by Lane collection and created several other partnerships ranging from camping equipment maker American Recreation Products to juvenile products maker Cosco, Inc. By and large, the company has done well to apply its brand in a dominant strategy with partner brands that are lesser-known in the consumer eyes. For example, rather than marketing a line of eyewear called the Signature Eyewear Company Eddie Bauer collection (Signature who?), the collection is appropriately called Eddie Bauer Eyewear, leveraging the brand's recognition and assets. Where the partner brand is on a more equal plane with the Eddie Bauer brand, it becomes more visible but still (mostly) remains in a subordinate position to Eddie Bauer, such as Eddie Bauer Lifestyles by Lane.

When a well-planned brand identity strategy is created and applied to licensing strategies and agreements, the licensed brand can successfully break out of its own niche and into others, therefore increasing its recognition with consumers. A company can get into much trouble with this approach, however, if a brand identity strategy is not well thought out or consistently applied. This can happen if names and visual identities are created at random (usually by multiple managers and agencies) with little relevance to the brand's total nomenclature. The result can be brand fragmentation, dilution, and, worst of all, a loss in public understanding and interest.

Technology Ingredients

In 1989 Intel's marketing manager decided to make IT managers more aware of the microprocessor Intel produced as the engine to computers. The approach was successful, and soon the PC industry was on-board to convert to the 386SX processor. There was one small problem. Intel assumed that there would be no legal challenges to promoting this alphanumeric name as a brand. But it soon learned differently. Trademark law then and now still sees alphanumeric "names" as generic and not defendable. Therefore anyone and everyone could use the number-letter combination by simply attaching the company name to it. Another problem was that in order to build awareness of the processor to PC buyers as well as IT managers, the company brand name needed to gain better awareness. At the time, Intel had invested billions of dollars in research and development to create the most cutting-edge and reliable technology. The company wanted to get its brand name out there to make consumers aware of what separated Intel from the pack. A new marketing approach was needed. The Intel Inside program was officially launched in 1991 and paved the way for an entirely new approach to brand identities and what would even warrant a proprietary brand. Transforming a semiconductor company that was well known in the industry but not at all known to end users is a coup in and of itself. Creating brand awareness of the company through the "ingredient" supplied to PC manufacturers but invisible to end users created a major phenomenon. Today the Intel brand enjoys brand awareness and recognition on the level of Coke and McDonald's. The Intel processor is a main gauge used by consumers to decide which PC to buy. It's even an indicator of time: you know, the year that the Pentium III was standard versus the Pentium IV.

To get to that place, the Intel marketing team studied the successful ingredient branding and marketing efforts of Teflon, Dolby, and NutraSweet and began to apply the practices to the computer industry. Intel's advertising agency Dahlin Smith and White recommended using the tag line "Intel, The Computer Inside" for their subsequent advertising. Later this was condensed to the now infamous Intel Inside.

What the original tag line did was begin to position not only the Intel company name but the role of the processor within a computer. In 1991 the Intel Inside co-op marketing program was launched. In essence it was an incentive-based cooperative advertising program open to all computer manufacturers to pool money to create advertising for their product along with the Intel Inside logo. Not only did the program allow everyone's advertising dollars to go further, but the print ads quickly positioned the role of the processor in the minds of consumers and promoted Intel as the latest "must have" technology. The program was a whopping success and set the tone for additional Intel advertising using the latest special effects and signature audio ID (in this case a five-tone medley) to further position and promote the Intel brand and its relationship to PCs.[5]

As time marched on, a new strategy of going from the alphanumeric system of naming processors to creating distinctive, proprietary brand names both broke and created new rules of engagement about naming technologies. The Intel Pentium processor was the first to be created modified by roman numerals—a takeoff on the software industry's use of version numbers. Today the Intel Xeon and Itanium are additional brands for workstations and servers, while the latest Pentium has migrated to the Intel

Pentium IV Processor M—"M" indicating mobile or laptop-specific.

Lest you think the marketing magic was (and is) all done on a shoestring budget, think again. As we've indicated before, creating and building a world-class brand takes time and money. While Intel achieved success at the virtual speed of light in the 1990s, the cost of doing so was estimated at around $7 billion.

Following Intel Inside's success, many technology companies have followed suit in applying what we refer to as the technology (ingredient) branding model. Many companies have developed proprietary technologies that are services for other companies and end users. Internet companies such as Google and Akamai have successfully deployed these models and are a couple of the lucky dot-com survivors. The B2B trend that emerged out of the dot-com craze was an interesting one. While the notion that business-to-business brands were different than traditional brands (because of the markets and lack of traditional consumer channels) seemed logical, we were never convinced that B2B brands warranted a different approach to identity creation. They are different in brand building, yes, but not in identity creation. From that particular perspective, the B2B uniqueness is expressed within the initial positioning strategy: namely, the audiences, markets, possible communication attributes, positioning statement, specific objectives, and technical parameters. This is as true for B2B and other technology brands as it is for ingredient brands.

The general approach is similar to creating any other type of traditional brand. The strategic and creative details make the process, and therefore the outcome, different. The strategic details guide the creative process to be appropriate for the nature of that particular brand to be created. Think of it as programming the DNA strands with the appropriate elemental information so that the rest of the identity fleshes out with maximum efficiency and minimum effort based on how the DNA guides the creation. So now that it's apparent that creating brands for ingredients and technologies is similar to creating traditional brands, keep in mind that what makes ingredient and technology brands truly work is the brand-building process. This is where cooperative advertising and different marketing and public relations techniques can really make or break a brand.

8

APPLYING THE
KNOWLEDGE

You now know the difference between identity and image and will never again confuse the two. And you're also now a walking encyclopedia of brand identity, brand, branding, brand building, and any other *b* word. Are you ready to tackle your own project? Perhaps you're ready to oversee a project with the help of an outside agency or consultant, or perhaps you're an investment professional reviewing the state of a portfolio company's identity. Regardless of your position, this chapter is meant to assist you by providing a summary of the identity creation process. In this chapter you'll find several checklists to help you create or fine-tune an identity through the first three phases.

Choosing the Right Team

When you're looking for an outside agency or consultant to handle the identity creation process, it's important to know the scope of the project at hand, the time line, the internal resources (such as decision makers, in-house designers, legal counsel, project coordinators, recent research findings, etc.), and, of course, the budget. Budget can eliminate many agencies from the outset. There are large, well-known brand identity agencies that are capable of handling every phase of the process, therefore ensuring consistency of the identity at every step along the way. Some have overseas offices that may be helpful when dealing with large, international projects. The price tag on these agencies is generally quite high, and while there may be several senior-level consultants or principals who dazzle during a pitch, it may very well be the junior consultants who do all the work. The bottom line is, you need to find out all team members involved, their experience, and how they will work together. It's essential to understand an agency's proposed methodology and whether that particular methodology will fit well with your company culture and working style. References, of course, are also important to check out. We know from personal experience how a top-tier agency can impress a potential client purely based on the name brands it has worked on at one time or another. We encourage companies to ask detailed questions about the scope of the project worked on, how long ago it was, and whether there is someone you can contact who can provide feedback on how he or she felt about the experience and working relationship.

If the personality chemistry isn't right from the start, look for another agency. The task before you is usually long and intense from the very beginning. Personality differences will more often than not worsen down the road. If there are one or two personalities who present a challenge, ask if there are alternative team members available to interview. Be honest about what doesn't work for you and what does. Open, honest communication from the start can make a world of difference on both sides of the fence. Again, assembling the right team makes a tremendous difference in the working relationship, process, and outcome of a given project.

If a smaller agency or freelance consultants are more appropriate for the project, company culture, your work style, and your budget, go through the same interview process as you would with a larger agency. Focus on the prospective working partner's team members, experience, methodology, references, and of course check to see whether the personality chemistry is there. There are many smaller boutique agencies that focus on certain parts of the identity creation process, such as naming and research firms. There are also many freelance consultants who have big agency experience and contacts and can do a job as well as a larger agency for a fraction of the price. The advantage to small agencies and freelance consultants is they are often nimbler and more flexible and have a network of established relationships with other small agencies and consultants who can be brought into a project as needed. The downside can be a lack of consistency if too many different consultants are brought into a project with differing methodologies and philosophies. One person (a consultant or internal person) should always be appointed to ensure quality and consistency, therefore avoiding the dreaded "piecemeal work" syndrome.

One thing we do like to caution against is going with an agency that claims to "do it all"—brand identity, brand building, and a lube-and-oil change. Perhaps as this book is distributed, we will actually meet an agency that is capable of doing it all with excellent standards throughout, but so far we haven't come across one. There are not many people in the industry who have successfully bridged the identity and advertising gap. Most brand identity agencies and consultants don't claim superior knowledge in all fields, but rather, in what they specialize. For some reason there is more than one brand building agency that claims expertise in everything–from naming to media placement. Be sure to investigate all claims before entering into an agreement. One-stop shops are rarely what they appear to be.

Another important resource to look into is what we affectionately call the "brand police." Once the identity is created, launched, and implemented, the job of the brand police is to ensure that there are no violations of positioning or verbal and visual standards–and if there are, to quickly correct the violations. We have seen more than one company spend a lot of money on creating an identity only to have internal groups apply the identity incorrectly, inconsistently, or both. The brand police are also a helpful resource when internal groups take on new identity projects. They can provide identity guidelines and ensure that whatever is newly created fits within the already-established identity standards, to ensure consistency of the overall brand. One or more internal employees should serve as brand police. When monitoring newly created projects it's also helpful to engage a consultant either on retainer or on an as-needed basis to provide outside expertise and objectivity about how to keep the brand cohesive as it expands and contracts. At one point, Alycia was engaged in just such a role with a major telecom company, providing guidance on naming products, services, and features throughout the company. Because of the size of the company and the many internal divisions, it was quite advantageous for all parties to receive input and guidance on new projects. Therefore it ensured that the brand would not revert back to a fragmented state, as it was before a major nomenclature project was completed to clean up the piecemeal naming that had occurred for years.

The Phases of Brand Identity Creation

Here are the generally accepted phases of identity creation.

1. Positioning strategy
2. Verbal identity
3. Visual identity
4. Messaging (Can be created in tandem with visual identity phase)

5. Research (Can occur as an information gather-
   ing tool or validation tool at any phase)
6. Experiential identity
7. Brand building

The first three phases of identity creation are
almost always honored in this order. A project simply
cannot begin without a positioning strategy firmly
established and approved by the designated powers
that be within a company. Whether an identity is being
created or fine-tuned with internal resources or external, it's important to assemble a small team who will
oversee the project and approve work at each appropriate interval. Sometimes this includes middle management only, sometimes this includes the C level
team or founders (in the case of small and start-up
companies), and other times it's a combination team.
We always recommend that an ultimate decision
maker be involved. In our experience, approval by com-
mittee seldom works. We also encourage smaller versus larger teams.

Messaging, whether defined as nomenclature strategy, descriptor, positioning tag line, or copy points,
can often be created in tandem with a visual identity
phase. What does not work well is creating the visual
identity and name together. As we discussed in Chapter 4, because both the blatant communication as well

as subtle nuances of a name can significantly guide a visual identity, it's best to establish the name first and then visual identity. Remember, hundreds of names are created in the naming process, whereas the number of designs will be far fewer.

Research can be used as an investigative information-gathering tool or as a validation tool at any phase or phase interval along the way. There is no set formula as to when research is appropriate and when it is not. It depends on the company, the given project, and of course time and money. Keep in mind that even the most extravagant use of research does not guarantee successful results. Used appropriately, it is a guide, not the ultimate decision maker. Ultimately, gut instincts enter into the process, and there is a certain amount of simply making a choice and standing behind it with confidence that works best.

Experiential identity begins once the positioning strategy and verbal and visual identities are established. In this book we discussed the experience of a web site—by far the most common and ubiquitous form of brand experience today. The experience is the sum of all points of contact with the brand. Besides the web site, this could be a retail store, customer service, tech support, catalogues, the interiors of airplanes and hotels, in-store environments, interfaces and services for PDAs and cell phones, application interfaces, and others. There are many agencies in the United States and abroad who specialize in each of these categories. When evaluating firms, ensure that the lead consultants have a firm grasp of brand identity basics and how that extends to the creation and implementation of the experience.

Once the total brand identity is created, brand building can commence. Public relations, marketing in its many forms, advertising, and promotions should be fully apprised of the new identity and standards to ensure consistency when building the brand. There are many, many books on the market regarding brand-building philosophies and practices, and as you've now come to understand, this is not one of them. We placed brand building on our phase list to serve as a reminder of the mantra that motivated us to write this book: identity before image.

The rest of this chapter offers outlines of the first three phases. Use them as a checklist of essential steps along the way.

Phase One: Positioning Strategy

- Proposition
- Price points
- Target markets
- Audit of competitive practices

- Corporate relationships
- Target audiences
- Key features and benefits
- Audience messaging matrix
- Communication attributes
- Core essence
- Positioning statement
- Identity objectives
- Technical parameters
- Compare strategy components individually and as a whole to the building blocks of relativity, personification, assets, and differentiation
- Fine-tune as necessary

Phase Two: Verbal Identity

A. Establish Naming Brief Document

1. Project summary
   - Includes proposition, price points, target markets, corporate relationships, and any other appropriate positioning and background information
2. Partial list of competitive names
   - May include descriptors, positioning tag lines, and other relevant positioning messages as used in copy by direct or indirect competitors
3. Target audiences

4. Key features and benefits
5. Communication attributes
6. Core essence
7. Positioning statement
8. Naming objectives
9. Technical parameters
   - Include words and names to avoid and all previously created names
   - Designate primary and secondary foreign markets and languages to be aware of when beginning naming creation
10. Preliminary creative directions

B. Name Creation

1. Brief naming team
2. Create words individually and collectively
3. Critique what is created and set up a short list of names
4. Create more as necessary
5. Archive all names created in a master list of names

C. Trademark Availability Searches

1. Submit short list of names for preliminary U.S. trademark availability
   - In addition searches may include Dun & Bradstreet company name listings and other appropriate online databases

- Record information provided about un-
  available names; this can be in the form
  of the raw data provided by your legal
  team
2. Revise short list to reflect potentially available names
3. If not enough legally available names, go back
   to step B.

D. Cultural and Linguistic Analysis
1. Designate appropriate markets and languages
2. Provide names and project background to linguistic firm or internal international offices
3. Revise short list to reflect appropriate names
4. Record information provided about potential
   conflicts and/or connotations; this can be in
   the form of the raw data provided by the
   native speakers

E. International and Final U.S. Trademark Avail-
ability Searches
1. Submit as many names as appropriate (three
   to five minimum) for either:
   - Global searches: WISS (Worldwide Identi-
     cal Screening Search)
   - Regional searches: RISS (Regional Identical
     Screening Search)

2. Submit available names (two to three minimum) to final U.S. trademark availability searches

F. Final Steps
1. Select final name
2. Register final name with U.S. Trademark Office and foreign offices

Phase Three: Visual Identity

A. Establish Design Brief Document
1. Project summary
   - Includes proposition, price points, target markets, corporate relationships, and any other appropriate positioning and background information
2. Partial list of competitive visual identities
   - Includes wordmarks, logos, typography, primary and secondary colors, and any other relevant visual messaging used by direct and indirect competitors
3. Target audiences
4. Key features and benefits
5. Communication attributes
6. Core essence
7. Positioning statement

8. Design objectives
   - Include final name(s) selected or being considered
9. Technical parameters
   - Include all mediums in which the identity will live, such as print, TV, web site, PDA, cell phone, kiosks, retail environment, signage, trucks and livery, clothing and uniforms, etc.
10. Preliminary creative directions

B. Creative Exploration

1. Brief design team
2. Creative exploration of design concepts
3. Critique what is created and select key concept(s)
4. Create more as necessary
5. Create potential identities
6. Critiques what is created and select final identities
7. If fewer than two or three identities selected, continue exploration
8. Archive all designs created

C. Design Refinement

1. Refine selected identities (minimum 2)
2. Refinements can be based on color, typography, size, etc., or made to combine elements from two or more different designs

D. U.S. Registration Searches

1. Submit visual identities for preliminary U.S. registration searches
   - Record information provided about potential conflicts; this can be in the form of the raw data provided by your legal team
2. If conflicts with all designs submitted, go back to creative exploration and/or refinements

E. Cultural Analysis

1. Submit visual identities for cultural analysis in designated markets
   - Record information provided about potential conflicts and/or connotations; this can be in the form of the raw data provided by the natives interpreting visual message

F. International and Final Registration Searches

1. Submit visual identities for country-by-country international registration searches and final U.S. registration searches
   - Record information provided about potential conflicts and/or connotations; this can be in the form of the raw data provided by legal counsel

G. Final Selections

1. Select final identity based on legal and cultural outcome

2. If identities encounter conflicts, go back to creative exploration and/or refinements and commence legal and cultural searches once more

H. Design Adaptation

1. Adapt visual identity to prototypes such as business cards, letterhead, multimedia environments, etc.

I. Design Guidelines

Create print and/or interactive reference handbook from internal teams and media agencies that include the following:

The Corporate Identity   Brief overview and explanation of the identity system that may include the strategy, rationale, and vision behind the design system. This section helps clarify why the system was created and can provide education of value to new employees. Part of the message should incorporate why it is important to follow these guidelines and the power behind a consistent application of the identity to build a brand.

Signature System   Identifies each of the core elements of the core identity by name similar to the example in Figure 4–1. Explains the various parts of the identity and provides a common vocabulary for people to use for consistency.

The Tag Line   Explains the positioning tag line and the rationale behind its selection and its usage. If the brand is or will be marketed internationally, there may be several translations or native script versions that should be demonstrated and rules provided for appropriate application.

Color Specifications   Identifies the specific colors for each of the identity elements. The formulations for CMYK and RGB should be listed as well as the Pantone equivalents. If there is significant meaning behind the colors, such as from a country's flag or historical relevance, or perhaps that the red represents speed, this should be articulated in this section.

Typography   Identifies the specific typeface(s) used in the identity wordmark and tag line. Quite often a standard typeface is manipulated to make it more distinctive and proprietary. This needs to be clearly articulated so that all those creating or implementing designs will know that they must use the supplied reproduction art versus trying to use the original typeface. In addition, there may be additional complementary typefaces for marketing materials, signage, and correspondence that must be indicated. Remember that if these typefaces are not a default font (provided on your machine) in Mac or Windows, they should be provided as loadable fonts. There may also be rules included as to when and where these additional typefaces should be used.

Alternative Applications Provides a set of standards for applying the identity in unique situations such as one color, reversed, or on strange backgrounds. These standards should be fairly firm in tone so that people do not take creative license in their application.

Signature Don'ts Provides specific guidelines of what are not allowable applications, such as changing the proportions of any of the elements, usage of the tag line, changing the colors outside the approved system, placing the signature in a shape like a box or circle.

Signature Sizes Provides guidance for minimum sizes for printed versions with and without the tag line, different translations, or native scripts, and for web applications. If the brand is marketed internationally, the sizes should be indicated in metric as well.

Corporate Stationery Shows the correct positioning of the new identity, address, and contact information on letterhead, envelopes, and business cards. There may be several versions of stationery depending on the number of offices, countries, and translations required. If there are bilingual cards (generally two-sided) or letterhead, they should demonstrated as well.

Packaging Applications   If the identity appears on a consumer package, the guidelines will be more extensive depending on the complexity of the package based upon the number of sizes, flavors, ingredients, instructions, secondary packaging, etc. At a minimum the correct positioning and proportional guidelines can be explained. Mechanical art for products is far more complex than stationery or brochure artwork and should only be completed by skilled package designers an mechanical art work specialists. There may be a full set packaging guidelines above and beyond the corporate standards.

Basic Web Guidelines   Can be a single page with web color conversions and a homepage layout to a multi-chapter set of guidelines on each section of the site. This is an area that should be considered carefully as to who has access to the information.

Printing Specifications   Detailed layouts for stationery, brochures, packaging, and other marketing materials that include the placement of the identity elements, specific colors, dimensions, scoring and folding, and types of paper for printing the stationery system, brochures, and packaging.

Reproduction Art Should be included as digital files on disks or CDs for both Mac and PC. This should include the core identity elements, the alternative versions like one-color or two-color versions for multi-color identities or reversed versions, typography, and color standards. Also include the mechanical layouts for the stationery system, brochures, and other printed materials. Ideally, the entire design guidelines will be included on a CD for ease of use and updating.

Contact Information If your company has someone in charge of the identity in a marketing or design capacity, that person should be identified as the "go to" person for questions and clarifications of identity applications. His or her phone and email address should be listed.

Glossary of Terms A simple glossary of terms is very useful so everyone is on the same page. To many, this is a new vocabulary and there can be a lot of confusion. One page generally is adequate to educate novices to the design area.

ENDNOTES

Chapter 3: The Anomaly of Naming

1. David A. Aaker, *Managing Brand Equity*, New York, Free Press, 1991, p. 1.
2. Compiled from Unilever's web site: http://www.unilever.com
3. Compiled from Colgate-Palmolive's web site: http://www.colgatepalmolive.com
4. See http://apple2history.org/history/ah02.html. Original citation credited to Frank Rose, *West of Eden: The End of Innocence at Apple Computer*, New York, Penguin Books, 1989, p. 33.
5. See http://www.brandchannel.com/images/home/ranking_methodology.pdf. "World's Most Valuable Brands," survey conducted by Interbrand and published in *Business Week*, 2001. Rank compiled from web version.
6. Compiled from Kodak's web site: http://www.kodak.com.
7. Estimated percentages compiled at Landor Associates in the 1990s under the counsel of Mel Own, trademark attorney, Owen Wickersham & Erickson.

8. David Protz, "Czech Beer David Challenges American Goliath," published March 28, 2001 at http://www. protzonbeer.com/documents/27660-001488.html.

Chapter 7: Ingredient Branding, Technology Branding, and Other Interesting Formulas

1. See the Canderel web site: http://www.canderel.co.za/History.htm
2. See NutraSweet, listed at the following site: http://www.econ.kuleuven.ac.be/tew/academic/strateg/Students/Syllabi/
3. Ibid.
4. http://www.hoovers.com/co/capsule/4/0,2163,101064,00.html
5. http://www.intel.com/pressroom/intel_inside.htm

Index